Praise for *Tommy Douglas*

A GLOBE AND MAIL TOP 100 BOOK

"Lam … gives Douglas's incomparable career a thoughtful, balanced, lucid assessment."   —*The Globe and Mail*

"Lam's biography offers much detail about and insight into its subject."   —*Canada's History* magazine

"It's appropriate that Vincent Lam should author this contribution to Penguin's series: the Scotiabank Giller Prize–winning writer is also a practicing physician, and understands first-hand the legacy of universal health care that Douglas fought for in Saskatchewan and was later adopted by the federal government."   —*Quill & Quire*

"[Lam] has put in a Herculean research effort, which enables him to bring Douglas to life with scores of compelling anecdotes…. *Tommy Douglas* is easy reading, which is a testament to Lam's effortless style."

Praise for the Extraordinary Canadians series

"These books are not definitive biography; rather, they are opportunities to deepen the relationship between Canadians of the past and Canadians of the present. May this dialogue continue, so that today's biographers themselves will be the subject of the next wave of writers." —*The Globe and Mail*

"The concise books are a vivid, 'character-driven patchwork' of modern Canadian history made relevant to modern readers. In other words, no dry academic tomes allowed.... What's compelling about the Extraordinary Canadians series is that it draws you back to some of the original oeuvres—to Anne, to Carr's remarkable paintings or to Glenn Gould's Goldberg Variations." —*Vancouver Sun*

"Marvelous." —*Ottawa Citizen*

"Extraordinary Canadians features snappy, candid, highly personal sketches not meant to be definitive biographies. They are, instead, individual glimpses into the lives of some of the country's most prized achievers." —*London Free Press*

"Gorgeous little books." —*Toronto Star*

"[The] Extraordinary Canadians series, ably edited by John Ralston Saul, is … appealing because its subject matter is so varied, and the books are all written by people who either knew or took a personal interest in the famous Canadians they're writing about."   —*Calgary Herald*

"Entertaining, literary and informative."   —*National Post*

"Excellent."   —*Winnipeg Free Press*

"The concept of the series is a good one, especially the emphasis on brevity."   —*The Walrus*

"Don't be put off by the charming simplicity of format and language of these books. There's a depth and passion to them that is compelling."   —*Canada's History* magazine

"A series to collect and cherish. As ambitious a publishing program as has been seen in years, it is a reminder of how good a biography can be." —*The SunTimes* (Owen Sound)

PENGUIN

TOMMY DOUGLAS

DR. VINCENT LAM was born in London, Ontario, and grew up in Ottawa. His family is from the expatriate Chinese community of Vietnam. Trained in Toronto, he is an emergency physician and a lecturer at the University of Toronto who also does international air evacuation work and expedition medicine on Arctic and Antarctic ships. His first book, *Bloodletting and Miraculous Cures,* won the 2006 Scotiabank Giller Prize. Dr. Lam is co-author of *The Flu Pandemic and You,* which received an award from the American Medical Writers Association in 2007. His debut novel, *The Headmaster's Wager,* was a finalist for the Governor General's Literary Award in 2012. He and his family live in Toronto.

SERIES EDITOR:
John Ralston Saul

Tommy Douglas

by VINCENT LAM

With an Introduction by
John Ralston Saul

SERIES EDITOR

EXTRAORDINARY
CANADIANS

PENGUIN

an imprint of Penguin Canada

Published by the Penguin Group
Penguin Group (Canada)
90 Eglinton Avenue East, Suite 700, Toronto, Ontario, Canada M4P 2Y3

Penguin Group (USA) Inc., 375 Hudson Street, New York, New York 10014, U.S.A.
Penguin Books Ltd, 80 Strand, London WC2R 0RL, England
Penguin Ireland, 25 St Stephen's Green, Dublin 2, Ireland (a division of Penguin Books Ltd)
Penguin Group (Australia), 707 Collins Street, Melbourne, Victoria 3008, Australia
(a division of Pearson Australia Group Pty Ltd)
Penguin Books India Pvt Ltd, 11 Community Centre, Panchsheel Park,
New Delhi – 110 017, India
Penguin Group (NZ), 67 Apollo Drive, Rosedale, Auckland 0632, New Zealand
(a division of Pearson New Zealand Ltd)
Penguin Books (South Africa) (Pty) Ltd, 24 Sturdee Avenue, Rosebank,
Johannesburg 2196, South Africa

Penguin Books Ltd, Registered Offices: 80 Strand, London WC2R 0RL, England

First published in Penguin hardcover by Penguin Canada, 2011

Published in this edition, 2013

1 2 3 4 5 6 7 8 9 10 (WEB)

Copyright © Vincent Lam, 2011
Introduction copyright © John Ralston Saul, 2011

Manufactured in Canada.

LIBRARY AND ARCHIVES CANADA CATALOGUING IN PUBLICATION

Lam, Vincent
Tommy Douglas / Vincent Lam.

(Extraordinary Canadians)
Includes bibliographical references.

ISBN 978-0-14-316917-8

1. Douglas, T. C. (Thomas Clement), 1904–1986. 2. Saskatchewan—Politics and
government—1944–1964. 3. Canada—Politics and government—20th century.
4. Premiers (Canada)—Saskatchewan—Biography. 5. Legislators—Canada—Biography.
I. Title. II. Series: Extraordinary Canadians

FC3525.1.D68L34 2013   971.24'03092   C2013-900588-9

Visit the Penguin Canada website at **www.penguin.ca**

Special and corporate bulk purchase rates available; please see
www.penguin.ca/corporatesales or call 1-800-810-3104, ext. 2477

ALWAYS LEARNING   PEARSON

To Alexander, Sophia,
and Theodore

CONTENTS

John Ralston Saul

How do civilizations imagine themselves? One way is for each of us to look at ourselves through our society's most remarkable figures. I'm not talking about hero worship or political iconography. That is a danger to be avoided at all costs. And yet people in every country do keep on going back to the most important people in their past.

This series of Extraordinary Canadians brings together rebels, reformers, martyrs, writers, painters, thinkers, political leaders. Why? What is it that makes them relevant to us so long after their deaths?

For one thing, their contributions are there before us, like the building blocks of our society. More important than that are their convictions and drive, their sense of what is right and wrong, their willingness to risk all, whether it be their lives, their reputations, or simply being wrong in public. Their ideas, their triumphs and failures, all of these somehow constitute a mirror of our society. We look at these people, all dead, and discover what we have been, but also what we can be. A mirror is an instrument for measuring ourselves. What we see can be both a warning and an encouragement.

These eighteen biographies of twenty key Canadians are centred on the meaning of each of their lives. Each of them is very different, but these are not randomly chosen great figures. Together they produce a grand sweep of the creation of modern Canada, from our first steps as a democracy in 1848 to our questioning of modernity late in the twentieth century.

All of them except one were highly visible on the cutting edge of their day while still in their twenties, thirties, and forties. They were young, driven, curious. An astonishing level of fresh energy surrounded them and still does. We in the twenty-first century talk endlessly of youth, but power today is often controlled by people who fear the sort of risks and innovations embraced by everyone in this series. A number of them were dead—hanged, infected on a battlefield, broken by their exertions—well before middle age. Others hung on into old age, often profoundly dissatisfied with themselves.

Each one of these people has changed you. In some cases you know this already. In others you will discover how through these portraits. They changed the way the world hears music, thinks of war, communicates. They changed how each of us sees what surrounds us, how minorities are treated, how we think of immigrants, how we look after each other, how we imagine ourselves through what are now our stories.

You will notice that many of them were people of the word. Not just the writers. Why? Because civilizations are built around many themes, but they require a shared public language. So Laurier, Bethune, Douglas, Riel, LaFontaine, McClung, Trudeau, Lévesque, Big Bear, even Carr and Gould, were masters of the power of language. Beaverbrook was one of the most powerful newspaper publishers of his day. Countries need action and laws and courage. But civilization is not a collection of prime ministers. Words, words, words—it is around these that civilizations create and imagine themselves.

The authors I have chosen for each subject are not the obvious experts. They are imaginative, questioning minds from among our leading writers and activists. They have, each one of them, a powerful connection to their subject. And in their own lives, each is engaged in building what Canada is now becoming.

That is why a documentary is being filmed around each

subject. Images are yet another way to get at each subject and to understand their effect on us.

The one continuous, essential voice of biography since 1961 has been the *Dictionary of Canadian Biography*. But there has not been a project of book-length biographies such as Extraordinary Canadians in a hundred years, not since the Makers of Canada series. And yet every generation understands the past differently, and so sees in the mirror of these remarkable figures somewhat different lessons. As history rolls on, some truths remain the same while others are revealed in a new and unexpected way.

What strikes me again and again is just how dramatically ethical decisions figured in these people's lives. They form the backbone of history and memory. Some of them, Big Bear, for example, or Dumont, or even Lucy Maud Montgomery, thought of themselves as failures by the end of their lives. But the ethical cord that was strung taut through their work has now carried them on to a new meaning and even greater strength, long after their deaths.

Each of these stories is a revelation of the tough choices unusual people must make to find their way. And each of us as readers will find in the desperation of the Chinese revolution, the search for truth in fiction, the political and military dramas, different meanings that strike a personal chord. At first it is that personal emotive link to such figures which draws us in. Then we find they are a key that opens the whole society of their time to us. Then we realize that in that 150-year period many of them knew each other, were friends, opposed each other. Finally, when all these stories are put together, you will see that a whole new debate has been created around Canadian civilization and the shape of our continuous experiment.

Tommy Douglas cuts across that experiment: a young man who witnessed the most violent events of the Winnipeg Strike from a rooftop; a socially engaged religious figure; the social democrat who broke through to government; the father of single-tier health care; the only national leader to stand up against the imposition of the War Measures Act in 1970. In a sense he was the inheritor of Laurier's "Sunny Ways."

Vincent Lam, a powerful new force in our writing world, understands medicare, understands the strength of a committed believer, understands the nature of social justice. And he brings all of this to the biography of a man who balanced the power of the word with the realities of action. Douglas stands as a reminder that any of us can try to do the right thing.

My dream is for people around the world to look up and to see Canada like a little jewel sitting at the top of the continent.

—TOMMY DOUGLAS, 1951, TO HIS DAUGHTER SHIRLEY

CHAPTER 1

The Greatest Canadian

We should never, never be afraid or ashamed about dreams. The dreams won't all come true; we won't always make it; but where there is no vision a people perish. Where people have no dreams and no hopes and aspirations, life becomes dull and a meaningless wilderness.
—TOMMY DOUGLAS, FROM A.W. JOHNSON'S *DREAM NO LITTLE DREAMS: A BIOGRAPHY OF THE DOUGLAS GOVERNMENT OF SASKATCHEWAN, 1944–1961*

One night, after returning home late from the Saskatchewan legislature in Regina, Premier Tommy Douglas and his teenage daughter Shirley took their family dog out for a winter walk. Both father and daughter loved their late-evening walks under the clear prairie sky. Douglas would ask Shirley about school, tell her what was happening in the legislature, and show her the constellations. He loved the stars, and nature, though his work kept him at the legislature most of his waking hours. Their boots crunching the snow, Douglas said, "What a wonderful night. Look at the moon. One night, Shirley pet, you will go to the moon." It was the

1950s, and the notion of men on the moon might have seemed wildly speculative to some, but Douglas insisted that "in your generation you will go to the moon. Others will go first. They'll have it all arranged. People will be able to take trips to the moon."

This was Tommy Douglas—a visionary. As leader of the Saskatchewan Co-operative Commonwealth Federation (CCF) from 1942, premier of that province for seventeen years (from 1944 to 1961—the first socialist government in North America), the founding leader of the national New Democratic Party (NDP) in 1961, and the father of universal public health care in Canada, among other initiatives, most of Douglas's visions did not involve space exploration. They had everything to do with what Canada could be if Canadians worked co-operatively and concerned themselves with the welfare of their fellow citizens. In the Canada of his boyhood, universal health care, a charter of rights and freedoms, strong worker protection legislation, and other facets of our society that we now take for granted were the stuff of imagination and hope. Douglas helped to make many of them realities, demonstrating that ordinary people working for positive change could prevail.

IN 2004 Thomas Clement Douglas was voted "The Greatest Canadian of All Time" in a CBC Television competition, a sort of popularity contest without defined criteria. It put Douglas in the running not just with other politicians, such as Pierre Elliott Trudeau, but also with hockey players like Wayne Gretzky. Still, the fact that Tommy Douglas came out on top of "The Great One" tells us something about what Canadians value most about their country and how we see his contribution to it. Douglas won the premiership of Saskatchewan in a landslide, upset victory and reinvented that province. Later, when his influence was felt on the national level, both the humanist spirit and the practical benefits of the innovations that he championed profoundly shaped all of Canadian society in far-reaching ways.

Like many people in this country, I was influenced by Douglas before I even knew who he was, because of our medicare system, his best-known legacy, which was well established and an iconic example of what is Canadian by the time of my childhood. When I was a boy I knew that I wanted to be a writer, and that I also wished to engage in some other kind of work. I wanted to be in a profession that would expose me to humanity and that would allow me to earn a living without requiring me to be a businessman. In my native and beloved Canada, medicine was the perfect fit for me. I could serve people irrespective of their wealth (no patients would need to wonder if they could afford a doctor's care), and I would get paid without handing any patient a bill, so I went to medical school.

A SMALL-FRAMED MAN, with no wealth or family connections, Douglas influenced by means of words and ideas, which transmitted his particular mix of compassionate ideals and utter practicality. Around a table with colleagues, he listened more than he talked, digesting and synthesizing the reasoning of those around him. He was a magnetic public speaker—people drove for hours across the prairies to hear him. On a stage Douglas easily drew the whole room to him. He always began his speeches with a story or a self-deprecating joke. He won the audience over before he persuaded them of his message, which was always well thought out and rational. When he got into the substance of the speech, Douglas managed to be at once radical, sensible, and humane.

In his words he sought to communicate a rare and powerful magic: the infectious substance of practical dreams. He believed that if he and his fellow citizens could envision a better society, commit to that ideal and work for it, it could become real. The practical quality of the dreams was crucial, for Douglas had no interest in abstract theory. He wanted people to have dignified work for fair wages, access to humane social services like health care and welfare, and to live in a free and egalitarian society where self-fulfilment was possible for all.

The infectious nature of Douglas's words instilled the best kind of aspirations in those around him. He didn't want people just to blindly agree and follow him; he wanted to communicate ideas to them. It was for all people to evaluate and determine what they believed to be good for both themselves and their fellow citizens. He held that the only way a society could make genuine progress was for people to actively work toward what they believed in. Once, as an adolescent, Shirley Douglas asked her father what he would think if she decided not to vote for him when she grew up. He said, "Well, it's very good for people to decide for themselves who they would vote for, and they shouldn't vote for someone just because they're related to them."

AT ONE OF HIS LAST GREAT SPEECHES, at the 1983 NDP convention, he addressed his supporters when they had come to a difficult crossroads. Douglas was seventy-nine years old. Although he was weakened by cancer, his grin and his jokes were as bright as ever. The NDP had just lost the 1982 provincial election in Saskatchewan to the Progressive Conservatives and was making little headway in gaining federal seats. Addressing the unsettled crowd, he conceded to the delegates that things were rough, but then reminded them that things had often been difficult in the past and would likely be challenging in the future. He pointed out to them that many of the NDP's ideas—medicare, a decent pension plan—had been adopted by opposing political parties. Although political co-optation proved the worth of the ideas, Douglas recognized that it had disadvantages; the other parties often watered down the programs they adopted and left the NDP with a diminished platform. What was more important than whether they won the next election, however, Douglas told them, was that they continue to advance their ideals over the next fifty years, to build a productive, peaceful, and caring society.

Many delegates wept openly, knowing that this might be the last time they heard him deliver a speech. When he was finished speaking, the crowd rose and cheered. After five minutes of wild applause, Douglas sat down, but the crowd would not stop, and the noise grew louder. He eventually climbed on a table to shush them, which only increased the cheering and commotion. For twenty-three minutes, the outpouring of joy, gratitude, and admiration continued.

Those who were there knew that Douglas had lived his beliefs, and they loved him for it. It was the pursuit of these beliefs, and their expression through his life, that made Tommy Douglas in many people's minds a great Canadian.

CHAPTER 2

Practical Christian, 1904–24

I got along fairly well with crutches but when the winter-time came it was very difficult, and a Polish boy and a Ukrainian boy came knocking at the house with a sleigh, and told my mother that they would pull me to school and bring me back every day. This would be about 1914. These boys speaking broken English, the kind of people that some folks referred to as dagos and foreigners and bohunks, these were the people who came and took an interest in another immigrant boy. Otherwise I just wouldn't have got to school.

—TOMMY DOUGLAS, 1958, ON THE WINNIPEG OF HIS CHILDHOOD

Falkirk, Scotland, was a gritty industrial town close to coal-mining districts, and many of its men were employed by the blast furnaces, steel mills, and ironworks nearby. There, Thomas Clement Douglas was born on October 20, 1904. His father, Tom Douglas, was an iron-moulder at the Carron Iron Works. At the time Scotland was an important manu-facturing centre. It produced almost half of Britain's steel, and its finished products included ships, railway locomotives, and household goods. Tommy Douglas's grandfather, also named Thomas Douglas, owned two small stone houses in the town. He and members of his family lived in one, and Douglas's mother and father lived in the other.

Tommy's earliest memory was of his paternal grandfather reciting the poetry of Robert Burns by the fireside in the family's stone house. It was a religious home but not a harsh one. Tommy's mother, Anne, was a Baptist, and his father had been raised a Presbyterian. They often had visitors, and frequently the carpet would be rolled up and there would be dancing of the Highland Schottische and poetry recitations. Tommy remembered a wedding in his grandfather's house, the minister having the honour of the first glass of whisky. This was the way of the Douglas household—faithful but not dour. Douglas described his paternal grandfather as surrounded by "a welter of words." He recalled, "My grandfather had eight sons, all of whom seemed to like to argue even more than he did, and so there was a constant bedlam of discussion: politics, religion, and philosophy, any one of which could finally be solved by a quotation from Bobbie Burns." Not all such conflicts could be resolved by poetry, and when Tom Douglas cast his allegiance with the Labour Party, his Liberal father was furious and did not speak to his son for months. It was the birth of Tommy that reconciled the two men. Years later, grandfather Thomas made the grudging announcement that he too had switched to the Labour Party.

Tommy's maternal grandfather, Andrew Clement, drove a delivery wagon in Glasgow and sometimes let the boy ride with him through the city streets. Andrew had been an alcoholic in his youth, until he found a spiritual light in the Plymouth Brethren and became a quiet, gentle teetotaller. Later he became a Baptist. In Presbyterian Scotland, both the Plymouth Brethren and the Baptists were religious nonconformists, refusing to comply with the requirements of an established church. Andrew Clement also became a loyal supporter of the British Labour Party.

From his father's side Tommy inherited his dedication to the cause of the working people and his love of Robert Burns, learning much of the Scottish poet's work by heart. From his mother's side he inherited a theological skepticism nevertheless rooted in deep faith. Both sides of the family bestowed on him independent thinking, a tradition of intellectual curiosity and rigour, and a willingness to hold strong opinions.

Tommy was once asked whether he was born into a home that was poor, rich, or in the middle. He replied, "Poor and rich are relative terms," and explained that by Scottish working-class standards his family had been comfortable, and by middle-class standards it would have been called poor. The men in the family had the skills to earn a living, if there were jobs. "If work got scarce," he said, "even the best artisan would have quite difficult times ... [but] compared with the unskilled workers or people who had some misfortune, we were comparatively well off." His father went to work early: he believed in giving his employer a full day of labour for his wages. From childhood, then, Tommy viewed the world from the perspective of the worker. One of society's most important economic benchmarks would for him always be whether a working family could earn enough to live decently.

When the manufacturing economy in Scotland faltered, an era of expansion was under way in Canada. In 1911, attracted by the promise of better wages and working conditions, Tom Douglas and his brother Willie sailed to Canada, crossed the country by train, and disembarked in Winnipeg. They stayed at a rooming house on Disraeli Street, and went to work at the Vulcan Iron Works. In the spring Tom Douglas sent for his wife, Anne, their son, Tommy, and daughter, Nan. Another daughter, Isobel, was born soon afterwards in Winnipeg. At that time a frontier city of mud streets and frame buildings, it had a population of 150,000 and was both a regional economic centre and a jumping-off point for masses of new immigrants to Canada. Winnipeg was the most ethnically diverse city in Canada, as immigrants arrived from all over Europe to start a new life.

Tom was enthusiastic about the multicultural face of Winnipeg, and on the street where they lived, there were Germans, Ukrainians, and Poles, as well as two other Scots families. From a young age Tommy was encouraged by his father to embrace the ethnic mix in Canada. Naturally, this philosophy was conveyed in lines from Burns's poem "A Man's a Man for A' That." Tommy recalled, "He used to keep pounding it into me when I was a kid: 'You're playing with the Kravchenko kid. This is marvellous; this is what the world should be like. Sure, I can't understand the family next door, but you kids are growing up together, and you'll work for the same kinds of things, you'll build the same kind of world.'"

Tom grew onions and cabbages in the backyard of their rented house. A warm, helpful man, he often shared vegetables with neighbours and looked for ways to help people out. He prayed but did not attend church: ever since he had had an argument with the Presbyterian minister in Falkirk, Tom had concluded that the church was allied with the wealthy and against the workers. He read a great deal, believed that he had as much right as any man to form his own opinions on the issues of the day, and preferred to deal directly with God.

Tommy's mother, despite her husband's antipathy to organized religion, was an active participant in church activities. Anne was involved with several north Winnipeg churches, and volunteered at the Methodist All People's Mission, which operated under the guidance of Rev. James Shaver Woodsworth. He was a Methodist minister who disagreed with the church's emphasis on spiritual salvation over addressing the social injustices he saw all around him. His objections led him to try to resign in 1907, but he was persuaded instead to accept the superintendancy of the All People's Mission in the North End. The Mission offered English classes and helped recent immigrants who were trying to settle in a new country. From this base Woodsworth campaigned for compulsory education, the building of playgrounds, the establishment of juvenile courts, and other social welfare advances. He wrote two books calling for a living wage for workers and a more equal and compassionate society in Canada; *Strangers Within Our Gates* and *My Neighbour* were published about the time the Douglas family arrived in Canada. Woodsworth would later play an important role in Tommy Douglas's political career.

It was through the All People's Mission that Tommy was first exposed to the reformist thinking of the social gospel. The social gospel movement, which he later called "practical Christianity," grew up in response to the suffering of many at the dawn of the industrial age and alongside early-twentieth-century excitement with new ideas and knowledge. Its proponents believed that the Christian God was benevolent and concerned with the earthly welfare of humans rather than a God of anger and retribution, and that this God wished for tolerance of differences among people and the creation of a brotherhood of man on earth.

Social gospellers helped elect Keir Hardie as the first Labour MP in Britain, and built institutions like the Young Men's Christian Association (YMCA) in the United States. Though prominent in charity work, they argued that the most pressing task facing Christians was to influence governments to build societies in which social and economic justice would render charity obsolete. They embraced the future and the potential of using new knowledge to improve society, advocating in fields as diverse as co-operative economic development and urban planning to create good housing and parks, along with adult education to elevate the lives of workers. On the prairies, figures like Rev. Salem Bland saw that Canada could either become a weak imitator of the

United States, "ruled by millionaires," or pursue its own vision: "We need an ideal, before our resources are seized, while the country is young and our new cities are growing up … Our ideal shall be: Canada for the people! We need a new party, a party that will have what no present party commands—moral enthusiasm!" Woodsworth advocated a new co-operative model of industry, in which workers would participate, "not as slaves, not as jealous rivals, but as partners in a common enterprise."

Such was the table talk in Tommy's Winnipeg childhood. His Labourite father and Mission-volunteer mother had brought their young family to a booming frontier city with its unfamiliar languages and bold ideas, in which radical church ministers sought to shape their young country. About the shift in attitude among some clerics, Woodsworth declared, "The earlier distinction between sacred and secular seemed to have no meaning." The new perspective had a decisive influence on Douglas. He said later in his political career that in Canada, every major reform in the social order had drawn its impetus from the social gospel.

Douglas often went to the All People's Mission after school to play in the gym, to swim in the pool, and to read the library's books. He remembered seeing the quiet, bearded Woodsworth from a distance. "Here was a fellow who could have been in a big church, had been in a big church, working among the poor people.... My mother had a great regard for him." Woodsworth would come to be known as "the saint of Canadian politics" when he later entered public office.

A shadow fell over the Douglas family in these years, in the form of illness. Tommy suffered from recurrent episodes of osteomyelitis, a bone infection in one of his legs. An injury that had occurred in Scotland prior to the family's departure had never healed properly. Tommy had undergone several kitchen-table surgeries there, performed by a country doctor, with Tommy's mother, grandmother, and a neighbour as surgical assistants. These operations were unsuccessful, and the osteomyelitis recurred in Winnipeg. This ailment was the bitter aspect of Tommy's childhood. One of his most painful childhood memories was of being stuck in a hospital bed with his infected leg, listening to able-bodied children playing outside.

Tommy was hospitalized repeatedly for a total of at least eighteen months, but none of the operations or treatments he received as a patient on the public wards in Winnipeg cured him. The doctors eventually recommended that the leg be amputated. While his parents were considering whether to give their permission for the operation, Dr. R.J.

Smith, a renowned orthopaedic surgeon, was going through the public wards of the hospital with a group of students, and he took an interest in Tommy's case. There was no way that the Douglas family could pay for the services of this surgical specialist. He offered to take over Tommy's care free of charge, and asked only that he could use the boy as a teaching case.

Dr. Smith performed several operations, the leg was healed, and an idea was planted in a small boy's mind that stayed with him for a lifetime. He said later, "I always felt a great debt of gratitude to him [Dr. Smith] but it left me with this feeling that if I hadn't been so fortunate as to have this doctor offer me his services gratis, I would probably have lost my leg ... I felt that no boy should have to depend either for his leg or his life upon the ability of his parents to raise enough money to bring a first-class surgeon to his bedside. And I think it was out of this experience ... I came to believe that health services ought not to have a price-tag on them, and that people should be able to get whatever health services they required irrespective of their individual capacity to pay."

With the onset of the First World War, Tom Douglas felt the pull of duty. Men like Hardie and Woodsworth advocated pacifism, but most of the socialists of that age heeded the call of the British Empire and enlisted. Tom Douglas had fought in the Boer War and knew the ugly realities of the battlefield. In this conflict he did not want to kill other men, and so, at the age of thirty-four, he joined the 12th Field Ambulance, a Scottish unit, rather than carry a gun. Anne and the children returned to live with the maternal side of the family in Glasgow.

Tommy remembers these as happy years. Life in Canada had been more difficult than the Douglases had anticipated, between the problems of earning enough money and the osteomyelitis. When they returned to Scotland, they thought they would stay there. However, once back, Tommy yearned for some facets of Canadian life. In Canada a boy could wander with considerable freedom, as long as his leg wasn't bothering him. In Scotland, however, Tommy discovered that much of the countryside was off limits, exclusive hunting grounds of the landed gentry. He said later, "Tramping over the hills and doing the kind of things that a boy wants to do, these you couldn't do in a large part of Scotland. This class distinction and this social framework had been fastened on so tightly." Tommy noticed the difference and disliked it.

In the streets of Glasgow, he fought his way into a gang so that he would have protection on the streets. He quit school just prior to his fourteenth birthday in order to help support his family. He went to work as an office assistant at a cork factory, and was so earnest and capable that the owner proposed that Tommy go to night school to learn Spanish and Portuguese. Then he could travel to Spain and Portugal and become the cork buyer for the business. The idea appealed to him—like many adolescents, he dreamed of travel and adventure.

During the war, however, Tom Douglas had himself transferred to the Canadian Army. Tommy recalled that when his father came home after the armistice was signed in 1918, he too was bothered by the class structure of his native land. "He'd had time to look around a bit, and saw the old class distinctions in Scotland ... this idea that you were in classes, and that the working-class boy didn't get up into the professional class and the professional class into the ranks of the gentry, and that the gentry would never expect to get into the ranks of the nobility, this irked my father." Tom and Anne Douglas decided to give Canada another try. In January 1919 Anne returned with the children to Winnipeg, where they would await Tom's discharge from the army to join them. Fourteen-year-old Tommy resumed his education, made sure his sisters were enrolled in school, and helped his mother get the family settled in a rented house. He bought a bicycle and used it to work as a messenger and errand boy. He switched from one job to another whenever he found something with slightly higher pay. Tommy never had a rebellious teenage phase: he was too busy doing what needed to be done for his family.

CANADA LOOKED BETTER than Scotland to Tom Douglas and his family, but Canadian society had its share of inequity. The prairies at that time were virtually a region of neocolonial dependency. The grain-based economy was developed as part of Prime Minister John A. Macdonald's National Policy in the late nineteenth century, an economic plan that was later extended by the Liberals of Wilfrid Laurier. After the forcible eviction of the First Nations peoples, the prairies were settled by farmers from other parts of Canada, the United States, and Europe. The farmers' produce was exported to the world's markets by railways whose owners controlled freight rates. The farmers financed their operations through banks based in Montreal and Toronto, and bought their consumer goods and farming equipment from eastern Canada at prices inflated by tariffs. Almost all the companies that controlled the prairie economy were based elsewhere and made excellent profits in that captive market. Many farmers were perpetually in debt, servicing one mortgage until it came time to sign a new one. The result was that the prairies had a large body of farmers who couldn't themselves get ahead but generated significant income for others.

Because the rural population came from a wide range of backgrounds, the fertile mingling of various traditions and political ideas made prairie politics especially innovative. From the late nineteenth century, prairie farmers tried to defend their interests through organized advocacy and farming co-operatives. These rural movements rose hand in hand with the social gospel, and parallel to the labour movement in manufacturing centres. Working people returned from risking their lives in the First World War with new solidarity and confidence. They had fought for freedom, and now they wanted their piece of it. Some worker activists called for a role in the management of industry. The Methodist Church issued a report in 1918 that stated, "We do not believe the separation of labour and capital can be permanent. Its transcendence, whether through co-operation or public ownership, seems to be the only constructive and radical reform." The Winnipeg that Tommy Douglas returned to as a young teenager, like much of Canada, was ripe for conflict between bosses and workers. At the beginning of May 1919, several months after the family arrived back in Winnipeg, Tommy witnessed the largest-ever strike in Canadian history.

Over the preceding months, workers in the building trades had become increasingly frustrated. The cost of living had jumped by 73 percent since the beginning of the war, while their wages had risen only 13 percent. They wanted better wages and the right to form unions and bargain collectively. The city's building workers called a strike on May 1. Metalworkers, who had long battled unsuccessfully for union recognition and had been foiled in three attempted strikes by the use of strikebreakers and legal action, joined the builders on May 2. Then Winnipeg police officers, streetcar workers, and telephone operators, who were also involved in a labour dispute, voted to join the strike, so by Thursday, May 15, the city of Winnipeg was effectively shut down. In a city of 200,000, an estimated 22,000 to 35,000 people were on strike. Business leaders spread the baseless rumour that Bolsheviks were behind the action, and the *Winnipeg Citizen* reported that the strike constituted a "determined attempt to establish Bolshevism and the rule of the Soviet." Rev. William Ivens, the editor of the *Western Labour News*, a newspaper that tried to tell the stories of the strikers, was arrested. J.S. Woodsworth, who by this time had left the church over his pacifist stance and was devoted to political activism, took up the post of editor.

The conflict came to a head on "Bloody Saturday," June 21,

when crowds of strikers gathered in front of Winnipeg City Hall. Tommy, his friend Mark Talnicoff, and a few other boys climbed onto a rooftop to watch the protest. It was a peaceful demonstration of strikers until the Royal North West Mounted Police appeared on horseback, along with a force of "special constables." The special constables had been hired, at twice the daily pay the regular officers had been receiving, to replace 240 Winnipeg police officers who had refused to abandon the strike. They were, in essence, hired thugs, and they wielded baseball bats and hoe handles against the demonstrators as the Mounties charged the crowd with clubs and revolvers. Bullets whistled past Tommy, Mark, and their friends on the roof. Below them, a man was shot dead on the sidewalk by the Mounties at the corner of Main Street and William Avenue. The strikers were dispersed, and within several hours the army had established control over downtown Winnipeg. That night Woodsworth was arrested for the editorials he had written supporting the strikers. By the end of June the strike had collapsed.

Bloody Saturday left a searing impression on Tommy. He had seen a peaceful protest crushed by the state in defence of corporate and government interests. "Whenever the powers that be can't get what they want," he concluded, "they're always prepared to resort to violence or any sort of hooliganism to break the back of organized opposition." Tommy would always see the world from the perspective of the common man trying to stand up for himself. Though he was to rise to a position of considerable influence, Tommy's allegiance remained always with the protester in the street rather than the Mountie who charged strikers on horseback.

Tom Douglas was discharged from the army and returned to Winnipeg several weeks after the strike. He was weakened in body and spirit by the war. He had been gassed and had witnessed the carnage of the trenches. He went back to work in the foundries and for the rest of his life would have bouts of despair. The only way Tom could confront his demons was by taking long solitary walks at night.

Tommy soon became a printer's apprentice at the *Grain Trade News,* and began to take night classes to improve his printing skills. A journeyman printer was a well-paid trades-man. His fellow printers were often self-taught philosophers and radicals, who were constantly reading the type they were setting and talking about ideas. The young apprentice read voraciously—at lunch breaks, on streetcars, and during his spare time. He read both adventure novels and political books. One book that influenced him greatly was *The Farmer in Politics,* by William Irvine, a preacher who had been elected as the Labour MP for Calgary East in 1921.

Irvine advocated the co-operative marketing of farm products and social Christianity as the radical alternative to capitalism.

It was at this time that Tommy began to develop what would become his legendary public-speaking abilities. He participated in local drama productions, recited Robert Burns at Burns nights, and sometimes other poems such as "The Highwayman," "The Legend of Qu'Appelle Valley," and "If," and performed monologues at dinners. One night Tom Douglas said to his son after a stage performance, "You did no bad." Tommy recalled, "That was as close as he ever came to giving me a word of praise. He might tell my mother that he was pleased, but he found it very difficult to tell me."

Tommy took speaking lessons one evening a week from a renowned elocutionist, Jean Campbell. Throughout his career, he could be heard pacing his words, drawing out his vowels, pausing dramatically for effect, and hammering a point home with his rhythmic staccato emphasis on key words and phrases. To listen to some of his famous political speeches is to hear a master of the form. Richard McLellan, Tommy's executive assistant on Parliament Hill through most of the 1970s, received public-speaking tutelage from Tommy. He recalls Tommy's coaching him with an eye on the clock, teaching him to hit certain points at certain times in a speech, and to pay attention to inflection. In addition to the importance he gave to the content of his speeches, he approached the delivery of a public address with a professional's acumen.

Another quality that became apparent in Tommy around this time was combativeness. Although his parents disapproved, he boxed competitively. He was tenacious in the ring and beat Cecil Matthews to win the Manitoba Lightweight Championship in 1922, a title he defended successfully the next year. He was modest in assessing his fighting career: "I was fairly average ... but I was fast on my feet and could hit fairly hard." In later years his political opponents would agree that he was fast and could hit hard.

It was in the early 1920s that Tommy began to wonder about his choice of career. As a fully qualified printer he was earning $44 a week. It was a good wage, and he was using most of it to help his parents pay down their mortgage. He wondered, though, if there was a greater calling that he was intended for. His social life was rooted in the Beulah Baptist Church on Kelvin Street. His younger sister recalled that Tommy went to church on Tuesday for Scouts, on Wednesday for prayer meetings, on Friday for a youth meeting, and three times on Sunday—two services and Sunday school. In addition to his stage performances and boxing, Tommy organized a church youth group and a Boy Scout troop, whose activities sometimes included weekend camping trips by bicycle.

Mark Talnicoff, who had watched the events of Bloody Saturday with Tommy, and who would later marry his sister, was one of Tommy's closest friends and part of these groups. On their weekend camping trips they sat beneath the stars and had long, intense discussions about the meaning of Jesus's teachings with respect to the social changes they were witnessing in the world around them. The social gospel movement spoke to the real problems of the working people of that time. Its new and idealistic ideas within the progressive parts of the Christian church were both a radical stream of thought in their time and the starting point of Tommy's political outlook. All of his early view of progressive politics was through the lens of a humanistic Christian faith. Thomas H. and Ian McLeod write in their biography *Tommy Douglas: The Road to Jerusalem*, "This movement expressed anger at existing conditions, but it also carried the hope, prevalent through the industrial nations, that people working in the service of God could shape a new world."

Mark and Tommy saw themselves as young radicals. They wanted to work for social change as an expression of God's will for men on earth and decided that to do so they should train for the ministry. Tommy knew that after several years of study to become a minister he would make less money than he was earning as a printer. His mother was a church-goer, and though his father was not, Tom had always hoped that Tommy would further his education. Both approved of his decision to enter the ministry. In the spring of 1924, he and Mark both enrolled at the theology program at Brandon College to pursue their calling.

tance that was compatible with the thinking of a young,
ndependent-minded Scottish immigrant like Douglas. He
as not only receptive to the critical and inquisitive think-
g that was taught at Brandon College, but also Professor
acNeill became his favourite teacher. "He recognized,"
id Douglas, "that you have to have answers to the ques-
ns about what we are here for, what we are supposed to be
ing.... How do you work with your fellow man to build
Kingdom of God?" Meanwhile, the head of the science
artment, Professor John R.C. Evans, provided Douglas
training in analytical thinking. Evans also taught him
to formulate and structure a speech, a skill he could
to his training in elocution. The ability to ask the right
tions, analyze the essence of a problem, and effectively
municate a synthesized perspective became Douglas's
leadership abilities.

he had done before Brandon College, Douglas soon
e involved in everything that interested him. He par-
ed in school drama, school government, and debating.
epresented the school at the Tenth Quadrennial
ntion of the Student Volunteer Movements in
t, the theme of the conference being "Wanted—
s for a Christian Internationalism." He was president
tudent body in his senior year. He led debating teams

CHAPTER 3

Boy Preacher, 1924–31

About seventy-five thousand men, mostly vagrants, were
living in the paper shacks or little huts they'd made out of
building materials, pieces of tin, anything they could get.
They were lining up at the soup kitchens as long as the
food lasted, begging, panhandling on the street, and
stealing whenever they got the chance.... There were boys
who had been bank clerks, medical students, and law
students.... One old fellow who had been a railroader
said something I've never forgotten: "Sonny, you can't do
anything to help us, there's nothing you can do. But go
back to this school of yours, and work, and see that this
doesn't happen again."
—TOMMY DOUGLAS, 1958, ON THE GREAT DEPRESSION

In 1900 missionary Baptists from Ontario founded Brandon
College on a plain near the Assiniboine River. It was intended
to be a post-secondary institution that would specialize in
both theology and liberal arts programs. It would also turn
out to be a forum for debate between the traditional and the
modernist thinkers within the church, and the intellectual
climate that Tommy Douglas found at Brandon College in

1924 was one that bubbled with both inquisitive thinking and theological friction.

Today our predominantly secular Canadian society assumes that religious thought operates outside of, or at most parallel with, secular concerns. At the time of Douglas's theological education, the predominantly Christian social framework of Canadian society was being challenged by new, critical ideas. Work by geologists and biologists had called into question the literal understanding of Creation. Academics, linguists, and theologians speculated about the historical origins of biblical tales such as those of Methuselah and Jonah's encounter with the whale. Some Christians were eager to explore the questions raised by this scholarship, while others rejected it. Such debate was waged vigorously, sometimes bitterly, at Brandon College, as elsewhere. Although nowadays Baptist churches in North America are associated with conservative and fundamentalist Christianity, at the beginning of the twentieth century they wrestled openly and often progressively with new interpretations of faith and dogma.

In 1922, the same year that the Scopes Monkey Trial in the United States challenged the right of schools to teach the theory of evolution (the Tennessee high school biology teacher John Scopes had so dared), Professor Harris Lachlan

MacNeill and several other Brandon acaden
with heresy by a group of Baptist minis
Columbia. Before a commission of
MacNeill was asked to explain his attitud
birth and the resurrection of Jesus Chrisr
he believed in them, but could not "ge
how they had happened. The commissio
MacNeill "believes in the fundamental
ural in the Christian revelation, but
faith and the liberty to investigate cer
He was acquitted, but his stance add
discord within the Baptist Union
Within a few months sixteen congre
Those that remained within it adhe
a modernist interpretation of their

A statement by the Union at tl
the intellectual climate that prev
when Douglas arrived: "We wou
ple of our denominational fell
every soul in the sight of God a
God ... a personal loyalty to Je
gramme as the acid test of all C
in the interpretations of religi
are consistent with the purst

s
i
w
in
M
sa
tio
do
the
dep
wit
how
add
ques
com
core

A
becar
ticipa
He r
Conv
Detroi
Builde
of the s

to frequent wins, but lost one notable match to Irma Dempsey, whom he began to court. Douglas supported himself by supply-preaching at country churches, waiting on tables, and delivering humorous monologues at local fundraising dinners for $5 a night. He later explained that some of his most successful monologues were "really a combination of corny jokes I still inflict on political audiences." The humour was often self-deprecating. "The best jokes," he said, "are always those in which somebody gets the better of you."

Douglas was a capable student and frequently won academic prizes, though he had competition from Stanley Knowles, who was destined one day to be a colleague in Ottawa. Knowles and Douglas would compete to see who could remember the most of a piece of poetry or prose. Blessed with a photographic memory, Douglas could cite facts and figures as if plucking them from the air. He was especially proud of winning the senior prize in his Hebrew class, which was composed of three students—him and two students preparing for the rabbinate. One of his college classmates remembered him as showing "a charismatic gift. He had a smile and a way of dealing with people, a rare gift of language and an ability to relate himself to whatever was going on as if it was his particular contribution."

In the midst of his studies Douglas agreed to take charge of Knox Church in Carberry: they couldn't find a Presbyterian minister and had to settle for a Baptist student. He took a special interest in invigorating the church's youth work, the Sunday school, and the Scouts. He also introduced his dramatic skills to the church: one of its notices announced his intention to "dramatize the Book of Esther." His sermons (and dramatizations) were so popular that it was often necessary to set up extra seating for evening services.

Carberry, though fewer than 150 miles from Winnipeg, was a different world. While Winnipeg's multi-ethnic North End was a hotbed of ideological debate, radical politics, and militant trade unionism, Carberry was a largely Conservative anglo-centric rural community. The local *News-Express* in the fall of 1927 printed an editorial that chided a teacher in Carberry for taking a few days off work to celebrate a Jewish holiday. At that time it was common for Canadians to hold anti-Semitic and racist views. After reading the snide editorial, Douglas made it known that he would preach a number of sermons on the Jewish people, and invited Carberry's two Jewish families to attend. People in the town recalled that he made it his business to challenge whatever anti-Semitic feelings lurked beneath the surface of the *News-Express's* pages. Then and later in his life, he felt quite free to state his opinions publicly, and to challenge people's religious and ethnic prejudices.

In 1929 Calvary Baptist Church in Weyburn, Saskatchewan, was looking for a new minister. Weyburn was only a generation old, and Calvary was a small white-painted church flanked by skinny, newly planted trees. Calvary had ties to Brandon College, where both Douglas and Knowles were in their last year. Both men auditioned for the job by preaching on alternate Sundays. The congregation chose Douglas, and Knowles found a job at a church in Winnipeg.

With a job to go to, Douglas asked Irma's father for permission to marry his daughter. The young couple were married in the autumn of 1929 by Mark Talnicoff, and moved to Weyburn on the cusp of the Great Depression. Knowles harboured no hard feelings about losing out to Douglas for the Weyburn job. He was the best man at Douglas's wedding, preached at Calvary during Tommy and Irma's honeymoon in Winnipeg, and organized the parishioners to greet the couple when they arrived in town. Douglas later reflected that when he went into politics several years later, and the Calvary Baptist Church was obliged to look for a new minister again, "some of the deacons were thinking that probably they'd made a mistake, and that they should have taken Knowles. But eventually Knowles became a CCF politician, too, and they'd have been stuck either way."

THE GREAT STOCK MARKET CRASH of October 1929 heralded the start of a worldwide depression. While those investors who had become rich in the soaring equity markets of the 1920s lost their shirts, many workers and farmers lost their pants, socks, and underwear. As Tommy and Irma, a young couple who looked more like teenagers than a pastor and his wife, settled in Weyburn, the price of grain collapsed, local businesses were shuttered, loans were called in, and family farms were foreclosed. Life for the farmers of Saskatchewan began to unravel. At harvest, grain fetched less than the farmers had paid for seed in the spring. Herds of cattle were sold for a pittance because farmers could not afford feed. Children did not attend school in the winter for lack of shoes to wear. The streets of Weyburn were lined with young men who had nothing to do. Saskatchewan was economically devastated.

Saskatchewan had grown rapidly during the preceding decades. Propelled by a healthy world demand for wheat, it had become Canada's third most populous province, with a strong rural base that comprised about two-thirds of its population. The Wheat Pool was formed in 1923 as a farmer-owned marketing system, and it—and they—thrived throughout the 1920s. The collapse of the world commodity markets wiped out the Wheat Pool's assets. Hundreds of thousands of Saskatchewan farmers, suddenly forced to sell crops at a loss, were drawn into a sinking spiral of debt. Several drought years added to their misery, for not only did farmers not have their cash crop, but they could not produce the vegetables, chickens, and dairy products with which they would otherwise have fed their families. Hard-working farm families, once proud and prosperous, found themselves at the mercy of Eastern banks, and dependent on the kindness of others for their survival.

In Weyburn, Douglas was known as the "boy preacher," with an irrepressible cowlick and wiry frame. His dynamic and thought-provoking work at the pulpit did not go unappreciated. The Calvary Baptist Church deacons wrote that "the Christian messages so ably interpreted and forcefully applied by Mr. Douglas ... were practical and helpful far beyond human ability to measure." He, however, was acutely aware that the spiritual guidance he provided from the pulpit did not help those parishioners who were being sucked into the economic whirlpool of the Depression. As the hard times wore on, while both federal and provincial governments were mired in inaction, an ever-larger number of the citizens of Weyburn and the surrounding countryside were struggling to make ends meet and sometimes failing.

Douglas had no intention of confining himself to polite company and an absorbed life of prayer. The vocal Christian left that had first drawn him to the ministry was trying to find practical ways to help people. As was he. The Calvary Church basement became a relief office and employment agency. Tommy and Irma were constantly buying for and giving things to people, and Douglas made frequent appeals to his congregation for more donations from those who were still able to give. He advocated before local town councils for greater assistance to the poor. As he became more deeply engaged in this work, he became increasingly aware that his charitable endeavours were addressing only the symptoms of the problem and not the underlying issues. A network of clergymen, teachers, doctors, labour activists, co-op organizers, and concerned citizens was forming around this realization, that their charitable efforts only soothed the wounds of a broken and unjust economic system—the unrestrained capitalism of the preceding decades. It was largely these people who would soon evolve into the Co-operative Commonwealth Federation, Douglas's first political party and the predecessor to the New Democratic Party.

At that time, with almost no services to support poor

families, their sons would often drift into gangs and criminal behaviour. One day the local magistrate rather craftily
called up Douglas and told him that he was going to deal
with the cases of eleven juvenile delinquents in court that
day. The magistrate lamented that they were repeat offend-
ers, and he would have little choice but to send them to the
grim Industrial School in Regina unless something could be
done for them. Would Douglas care to come to court to
watch the proceedings?

He went to the court and met the group of young offend-
ers. "Maybe it was because it was Monday," he later said,
"and I hadn't gotten over the Sunday sermon, but I ended up
having the eleven of them committed to my care by the
police magistrate. I wondered what on earth I was going to
do with them. I took them home. To march in with eleven
ragamuffins was quite a sight, and my wife, to whom I'd been
married for less than a year, just about went home to her
mother. She was a good sport, though." Tommy and Irma
found clean clothes, and Douglas organized odd jobs, classes,
and sports activities for the boys. He discovered that they
were very good at fighting but didn't know any of the rules of
boxing, which he tried to teach them. One Sunday, while he
was preaching, the boys burgled a store, and when the owner
complained to Douglas, he found them gorging on stolen

chocolate and smoking cigarettes. The minister hauled them into his office and gave them a long, powerful sermon, one of his best. When it was done, the boys began to cry. They promised to never behave so badly again. On their way out, one of the boys proceeded to return to Douglas his watch, knife, pen, and other items that he had stolen during the harangue. In 1945, when Douglas was touring the European theatre of war after becoming premier of Saskatchewan, he encountered the erstwhile thief again. He had become an army sergeant, and was assigned to Douglas as part of an honour guard in Holland. Over the years Douglas had the satisfaction of encountering many of these boys, who had cleaned up and done well for themselves.

The minister had become a social activist. He could hardly help himself: his concern for the disadvantaged and his particular affinity for youth were deeply ingrained from his own roots as a struggling immigrant boy. Also, he was never shy about telling people what he thought they should do. He had a knack for doing so in the most convincing way possible, whether he was cajoling boys away from a life of crime, or taking a local lawyer on a tour of some of the poorest households in Weyburn to persuade him of the genuine needs in his community. Giving practical assistance came as naturally to Douglas as encouraging people from the pulpit to do the same. This quality would endure. Irma's being a "good sport" would also continue. She was the steady foundation upon which their household was built, which made possible her husband's tendency to work from morning to night, always pushing himself to do more.

At that time churches across the country organized donations of food and clothing from British Columbia and Ontario. Many farmers in those provinces had crops they could not sell in the collapsed world markets, and they were willing to donate them to hungry Canadians on the prairies. Churches took collections to pay for freight so that train-car loads of apples and vegetables could be shipped to communities that needed them. It didn't make any sense to Douglas that in one part of the country there were farmers with produce they could not sell, while in another part were people who had no money to buy anything, and who wanted work but found none. Like many of his contemporaries, Douglas began to consider that many of these problems had been caused by the economic system. "The church was trying to do what it could about the effect, but what began to bother me was that we weren't doing anything about the cause."

Douglas asked questions about the economic crisis of the 1930s that seem as relevant today as they did in his time: "Why did this society break down? What was wrong with it?

Why was it that when you had a surplus of food and clothing and almost every known commodity produced by an advanced technological society, there were people who couldn't get decent houses to live in, couldn't get clothing to wear, and who couldn't get enough to eat? What had broken down? This is what made us all start to think." To try to learn some of the answers, Douglas decided that he would pursue further education. The Calvary church allowed their young minister his summers off to pursue his Ph.D. in sociology at the University of Chicago. In the summer of 1931 he was sent to do fieldwork in that city's hobo jungles, where he witnessed misery far surpassing anything he had seen in Weyburn. There were wastelands filled with thousands of young men similar to himself, the main difference being their bad luck. There were university students who had been forced to drop out for lack of money, who were ashamed to go home. There were skilled tradespeople who could find no work. The former workers and students of America had been cast into hopelessness by unfettered capitalism. Douglas was among those who concluded that the suffering of people during the Depression was man-made, and that the capitalist system responsible for the dire predicament was unable to fix the problem.

At the University of Chicago he sought out American

socialist academics and found that they had no practical answers. He concluded that there was a type of armchair academic Marxist who debated ideology and stopped there. Douglas recalled, "I went to their meetings. They spent most of their time debating whether or not, come the revolution, you would have communal feeding in the basements of schools, or whether we could have communal kitchens.... The fact that people didn't have anything to eat didn't seem to bother them at all." Douglas had grown up in an immigrant family that had struggled with the practical challenges of earning a living. As a pastor in Weyburn he had spent days at a time filling up bags with donated apples, carrots, turnips, and potatoes for the victims of the Depression. He was not interested in ideological speculation without action.

When he returned to Weyburn in the autumn of 1931, Douglas set about organizing the town's unemployed. He persuaded city council to provide an abandoned house that he made into what he called a "club room" for unemployed men. Today it would be called a resource centre. Coal was donated to heat the house, and a telephone was installed so employers needing workers could call. Douglas appeared frequently before the city council on a variety of issues. He presented school nurses' reports on children who were malnourished or had no shoes or clothing. He lobbied for more money for the unemployed. He sometimes found himself arguing with provincial relief officers who wanted to cut rather than increase benefits. As Douglas's activities shifted more and more from offering charity to demanding government action, some observers labelled him a dangerous radical. They confronted him, asking why he didn't get back into his pulpit and preach. He brushed off the criticism. "Whatever that may mean," he said, finding such questions about his proper task irrelevant.

Douglas had long since put aside the notion that his roles as a minister and as an advocate for the poor were separate. As far as he was concerned it was plain that God wanted faithful people to advocate for those in need, to confront suffering and injustice in concrete ways, and to convince people that they must assist with each other's struggles. However, he was beginning to bump up against the limitations of what he could do as a religious leader.

In the fall of 1931 a strike in the nearby Estevan coal fields broke out when management refused to meet the miners to discuss their working conditions and wages. An independent investigation had confirmed the miners' assertion that a miner could work long hours for months, but after deductions for lights, tools, and medical care might receive no payment at all. Douglas visited the striking miners and collected a truckload of food for them and their families. More and more he preached sermons with clear political implications, such as "Jesus the Revolutionist." He asked his congregation, "Would Jesus revolt against our present system of graft and exploitation?" Mine owners complained to the church's board, and "forbade" miners to attend his services. The strike ended when the mine workers tried to stage a demonstration and were met by police with guns and clubs. Three miners died, and twenty-three people were hurt. The wounded were brought to Weyburn. It seemed like a repetition of the police violence that Douglas had seen from a rooftop with Mark Talnicoff during the Winnipeg General Strike.

The Calvary church was part of the movement of socially active and politically progressive churches in western Canada. Members of the congregation had a progressive outlook and supported their pastor. Theirs was not a universally shared perspective, however, and Douglas was often criticized by more conservative colleagues. A fellow minister once argued with him that God made the rich so that they would learn benevolence and the poor so that they would learn gratitude. Douglas was outraged. "To me, this was sheer blasphemy ... I'm not a fit member of the Kingdom if someone else is undergoing misery or carrying burdens and

I don't attempt to help that person." There were also ministers in Weyburn who, though they quietly approved of what Douglas was doing, declined to participate in similar activities because they worried that their congregations might not be supportive.

Douglas had no such fear. For him, social activism was both an essential and a growing part of his calling as a preacher. Around him, good people had been thrown into the meat grinder of an economic depression, the apparent consequence of a greedy and exploitative economic system. In his view, speaking out against injustice and advocating for the poor was God's work on earth. With his Scottish father's sense of independence, his own fighting spirit, and Burns's immortal "A Man's a Man for A' That" ingrained in his conscience, Douglas concluded that God's fight was his fight, and simply ignored those who told him otherwise. Allan Blakeney, NDP premier of Saskatchewan from 1971 to 1982, later recalled that "when he got into politics, he didn't change his message, he changed his pulpit."

CHAPTER 4

Reluctant Candidate, 1931–35

> I got a visit from the superintendent of the Baptist
> Church for the West.... I said, "Many people here have
> been pressing me to run again. I don't want to run. On
> the other hand, I've seen the party build up and I hate to
> walk out and leave it." He said, "Leave it." Then he made
> the great mistake, saying, "If you don't leave it, and if you
> don't stay out of politics, you'll never get another church
> in Canada, and I'll see to it. The board has given me
> authority." I replied, "You've just given the CCF a
> candidate."
> —TOMMY DOUGLAS, 1958, ON HIS DECISION TO RUN FOR
> PARLIAMENT IN 1935

Despite the Depression, Tommy and Irma enjoyed their
years in Weyburn. They were active and popular. Irma sang
in the church choir, worked in the church women's group,
and attended local gatherings with her husband. She took up
the expected role of a pastor's wife and ran their house with
unfailing calm and competence.

Douglas and two other local ministers started a boys'

group for recreational and athletic activities. They organized sports and outings. He gave instruction in boxing, debating, and public speaking as well as lectures from his own university texts. Many of the boys were fresh out of high school and would have liked to continue their studies but had no money for university. Douglas wanted to keep the idea of education alive for them. The boys' group was popular despite some parents' reservations about the "radical leftist" minister. It must also have been inspiring because three of the boys became ministers and another two became university professors. Douglas started a local theatrical society and acted in plays. He even boxed in some of the matches arranged by the local boxing club. The family bought a house near the church and found an abandoned Model A Ford in the garage. They got it running, the church boys painted it green, and Tommy and Irma often took it to Carlyle Lake for holidays, where they eventually bought a cottage.

Because of his interest in helping the poor and vulnerable, his position as a Baptist minister, and his facility with words, Douglas was often asked by a farm group, the United Farmers of Saskatchewan, to speak at their meetings. Soon he found himself heading some of their delegations to Regina to speak to Premier James T.M. Anderson about the deplorable conditions on farms and the daunting economic obstacles that farmers faced. Some of the organization's leaders had begun to wonder whether there was some way that they could join forces with labour. In early 1932 the United Farmers asked the "boy preacher," who they knew would be sympathetic, to help them connect with labour groups.

Douglas had no experience in either labour organization or political advocacy, but he remembered Woodsworth from his time in Winnipeg and had fond memories of the All People's Mission there. Woodsworth was now in Parliament in Ottawa, and Douglas decided to write to him, hoping the older man would offer some useful advice. Woodsworth was deeply engaged in progressive politics and labour issues. Soon after his arrest and subsequent release during the 1919 Winnipeg General Strike, he had become involved in organizing the Manitoba Independent Labour Party. In December 1921 he was elected as the Independent Labour Party Member of Parliament for Winnipeg North. The first bill Woodsworth proposed in Parliament called for a system of unemployment insurance, which did not then exist. He would spend the next two decades advocating for unemployment insurance, old-age pensions, and other measures to assist the worker, the farmer, the immigrant, and the poor. In 1925, when the Liberal Party under Mackenzie King had a minority government, the narrow balance of power rested with two MPs—Woodsworth and Abraham Heaps, the sole other Labour MP. Woodsworth and Heaps made it clear to King that their support of his government depended on his amending the Immigration Act, the Naturalization Act, and the Criminal Code in ways they had tabled, and taking action on unemployment insurance and pensions. King agreed to act on all their conditions except unemployment insurance, which he believed too many members of his caucus would balk at. Woodsworth and Heaps were well aware of King's slippery ways and pressed him for written assurance of his commitment, which he gave them in a letter that Woodsworth subsequently read into Hansard.

King offered Woodsworth a cabinet post as minister of labour, but he refused it, preferring his independence. It was not until 1927 that the first Old Age Pensions Bill was passed into law, and though it offered only meagre benefits, it was nonetheless a victory for Labour. Woodsworth was already establishing the mechanism with which the CCF, and finally the NDP, would often come to exert influence at the federal level—through holding the balance of power in minority governments, and using this to advance sensible, progressive proposals.

In 1925 Woodsworth called for a nationalized system of

banking and government control of the issuance of currency and credit, with the removal of this power from private corporations. He contended that money supply should be managed for national interests rather than private profit, saying that in this "we face the larger question as to whether or not parliament is to be sovereign, as to whether or not the people are to be sovereign, or whether we have not had our liberties filched from us without most of us having been aware of what has taken place." In 1938 this line of thinking reached fruition in government. King nationalized the Bank of Canada, saying, "Until the control of the issue of currency and credit is restored to government and recognized as its most conspicuous and sacred responsibility, all talk of sovereignty of Parliament and of democracy is idle and futile."

When Woodsworth received the letter from Douglas, he was already working to build the CCF, Canada's first leftist national coalition. By coincidence, at about the same time, Woodsworth also received a letter bearing a similar inquiry from M.J. Coldwell, who also hoped that workers could gain a stronger voice through an alliance between farm and labour interests. Woodsworth suggested that Coldwell and Douglas connect. After all, they were both in Saskatchewan and could help each other out.

Major James William Coldwell (usually known as M.J., Major being his actual first name, which he disliked), an English immigrant, was a school principal in Regina and a Labour alderman. He was also the president of Regina's Independent Labour Party, had recently organized a conference of western labour interests that Woodsworth had attended, was deeply committed to the advancement of social justice and the defence of civil liberties, and was recognized as a rising political star. Coldwell's assistant principal, Clarence Fines, was the treasurer of the Regina Independent Labour Party. Douglas invited Coldwell to speak in Weyburn, which he agreed to do. When he came to town, he called at the Douglas house. Irma opened the door and Coldwell asked her, "Is your father home?" She was delighted by this greeting, and Douglas would repeat the story on hundreds of political platforms for years to come. Their meeting marked the start of a lifelong friendship. Coldwell visited several times to speak at picnics and meetings in Weyburn, and soon helped Douglas to organize the Weyburn Independent Labour Party, with Douglas as founding president. Later in life Douglas reflected, "At no time did I make a definite decision to go into politics. It was a cumulative conclusion."

The Saskatchewan Independent Labour movement was

never large. It might have had five hundred members at its height, appealing to both farmers and workers. It was Douglas's introduction to both politics and the people who would be his colleagues and supporters for decades to come. The movement achieved its greatest impact as a result of a weekly talk that Coldwell gave from Regina on CKRM radio. The station charged $6 for each fifteen-minute broadcast. Clarence Fines scrounged donations to pay for Coldwell's broadcasts. Fines's attention to the practical aspects of organization was the ideal complement to Coldwell's elegant way of speaking and his high-minded ideas. Fines would later play a similar role as the foil to Douglas, as the sharp businessman out to make or save a buck for a socialist government, the heavy to Douglas's glad-handing enthusiast.

In the spring of 1932 the economy was paralyzed. Suffering was widespread on the prairies, with nothing resembling what today we would call a social safety net. The United Farmers and Independent Labour jointly confronted the provincial cabinet on the issue of farm foreclosures. In July they established a formal partnership called the Farmer-Labour Party. The Weyburn Independent Labour Party organized public meetings, with topics such as "Socialized Medicine" and "Scrip Money." Some of the economic proposals were completely impractical, the speakers having the luxury of speaking freely without being in power. Other proposals of that time have since become features of Canadian life—unemployment insurance, universal health care, and old-age pensions.

While Douglas was increasingly involved in these political developments, he also explored a topic that may be the ultimate misguided expression of government involvement in society and social planning. He was working on his master's thesis in sociology by correspondence from McMaster University, having decided to put off his Ph.D. His thesis, "The Problems of the Subnormal Family," was an argument for a program of eugenics. In case studies drawn from around Weyburn, Douglas documented twelve "immoral or non-moral women" and their two hundred children and grandchildren. Collectively the group had high rates of sexually transmitted disease, mental illness, and police involvement. Douglas wrote, "Surely, the continued policy of allowing the subnormal family to bring into the world large numbers of individuals to fill our jails and our mental institutions, and to live upon charity, is one of consummate folly." The solution, he suggested, was that couples should be certified as to their mental and physical fitness before marriage. "Subnormals" would be segregated in state farms or colonies, and the "mentally defective and incurably diseased" would be sterilized. The thesis showed Douglas's enthusiasm for changing the world through science, planning, and government intervention. It also showed his readiness as a young man to cast a judgmental eye on his fellow citizens to a degree that now seems shocking from a man who, as a politician, would later become one of Canada's staunchest advocates for humane social programs and the defence of civil liberties. A sense of Christian righteousness is in evidence, as well, in his condemnation of a group of largely unwed mothers.

It must be pointed out that Douglas's thesis reflected the preoccupations of academic sociologists and psychologists at the time. The eugenics movement had been growing in influence for a generation, and included supporters such as George Bernard Shaw and others in the British socialist movement. In 1928 the United Farmers' government in Saskatchewan had passed the Sexual Sterilization Act and applied it frequently to inmates of provincial institutions. The Human Betterment League in California was sterilizing some of its citizens. We now know that there is no scientific basis for the "science" of eugenics, but at the time neither its falsity nor its defects from a human rights perspective affected its popularity. To the modern observer such notions are abhorrent. At the time some who imagined a better world thought that controlling reproduction would serve their aims.

What people do with power speaks more profoundly of their true nature than their youthful speculations. Years later, with the benefit of further consideration and the horrors perpetrated by the Nazis made known to the world, Douglas eschewed any support for eugenics. His actions in office made this clear. When the CCF government was elected in Saskatchewan in 1944, and Douglas became minister of health, he reviewed two proposals that the government undertake a limited program based on eugenics. He rejected them completely and instead promoted a system that offered more therapy for the mentally ill and vocational training for the mentally handicapped.

IN JULY 1932 the long-held dream of J.S. Woodsworth for a national left-wing political party became a reality. In Calgary, Labour Party delegates, United Farmer representatives, and the rail union formed an alliance with an agreed-upon statement of principles, and a new name, the Co-operative Commonwealth Federation. The CCF was born. A year later, they held their first national convention in Regina, and adopted a policy statement, the Regina Manifesto.

The Regina Manifesto spoke a language that reflected the tumult of its time, a world reeling from economic catastrophe: "When private profit is the main stimulus to economic effort, our society oscillates between periods of feverish prosperity in which the main benefits go to speculators and profiteers, and of catastrophic depression, in which the common man's normal state of insecurity and hardship is accentuated. We believe that these evils can be removed only in a planned and socialized economy." There is a quality of déjà vu to these words at the time of this writing, as the world economy in the early part of the twenty-first century has been dominated by euphoric booms of speculative capitalism and by gut-wrenching economic busts.

Many parts of the Regina Manifesto, though decidedly idealistic in 1933, now occupy the mainstream of Canadian values. The Regina Manifesto upheld the rights of religious and ethnic minorities, called for a Canadian central bank, denounced protectionist policies, and recommended a coordinated approach to trade. The Manifesto called for a Canadian constitution and a charter of rights. This document advocated many of the major legislative reforms that would be enacted in Canada in the ensuing decades, including unified national workplace standards, publicly funded health care, unemployment insurance, and adequate public pensions (the Old Age Pension plan adopted in 1927 by the King Liberals was a bare start). By the 1980s all these proposals had become reality, in large part due to the work of the CCF and its successor, the NDP.

Other components of the Manifesto have not been realized, despite their central importance to the CCF at that time. The authors of the Manifesto envisioned a strong network of Crown corporations, a regulated economy that was a mix of private and public enterprises, the active participation of workers in the management of industries, and a foreign policy focused on disarmament and world peace. The ideal was that "we aim to replace the present capitalist system, with its inherent injustice and inhumanity, by a social order from which the domination and exploitation of one class by another will be eliminated." The means to this liberation would be "a planned economy ... owned and controlled by the people," in which the guiding principles would be to satisfy citizens' needs rather than to generate private profits. Douglas was able to attend only the last day of the convention, but he saw enough to call the gathering "the finest thing I have ever seen." He said of this heady time, "There were those who believed that our present economic system was un-Christian, was anti-social, was harmful to all the traditions of humanitarian values." For Douglas the Manifesto was a vision of God's work to be done on earth.

The Manifesto would become a touchstone for people from various political perspectives. A last-minute addition to the document stated, "No C.C.F. Government will rest content until it has eradicated capitalism and put into operation the full programme of socialized planning." This was to become its most notorious text—used by those outside the CCF to condemn it, and used by the left within the movement to complain that the cause was being watered down by the CCF and NDP governments that failed to live up to it.

A PROVINCIAL ELECTION was called in Saskatchewan in 1934. The Liberals were expected to oust an unpopular Conservative government that had done little to help people in their hardship. In Weyburn the Liberals nominated a popular local physician, Hugh E. Eaglesham, whom Douglas described as "a very fine old family doctor who had brought half the people in our community into the world." Douglas was focused on his continued studies in sociology and on his work as an activist minister. Tommy and Irma's first daughter, Shirley, arrived in 1934, a bright, happy child whom the Calvary congregation adored. No one especially wished to stand as the CCF candidate. There did not seem to be even a remote chance of winning, and workers feared that being a CCF candidate would cost them their job. When no one stepped forward, it was put to Douglas by CCF and Farmer-Labour supporters that as the person who had brought the movement to the area, he had a duty to stand for office. With some mixed feelings, he agreed.

Of that first campaign Douglas later said, "I conducted it like a university professor giving a course in sociology. I had charts and so on, and I'm sure half the people didn't know what I was talking about. But I think it did some good. It laid the foundation, and we began to get people who understood the basis of our present competitive capitalist society, its monopolistic nature and structure, its basic weaknesses, and the fact it could never adequately solve the problems of distribution. A fairly good educational job was done." The CCF meetings were crowded and enthusiastic, and thousands would turn up, especially to hear Woodsworth. Despite his initial reluctance to get involved, Douglas was drawn into the excitement of a political race, the thrill of arguing for the ideas he believed in, and he admitted that by the end of the race, he thought that he would win his seat. In the end Douglas came third after Dr. Eaglesham and the Conservative candidate. When he conceded defeat in a speech on election night, he admitted his own disappointment and also foreshadowed his return to the fray, saying, "As Jonah said when he was swallowed by the whale, you can't keep a good man down."

When a federal election came in 1935, Douglas declared at first that he would not stand. His congregation at Calvary Baptist did not object to his running for office, but he liked being their pastor, had a new daughter, and was involved in socialist advocacy work in and around Weyburn. That was enough, he thought. Once again, he was urged by the local Farmer-Labour constituents of Weyburn to put his name forward. Douglas demurred, but his supporters insisted that there was no other suitable person in the region to represent the CCF. He received a letter from Stanley Knowles in Winnipeg, encouraging him to run, but he was still unsure. Only when the superintendent of the Baptist Church for the West threatened to end his career as a clergyman if he ran for federal office did he come to a decision. His fighting nature aroused, Douglas told the official that he had just given the local CCF its candidate.

These were years when Canadian elections were boisterous enough to constitute a form of public entertainment, and political meetings drew throngs who listened to speakers past midnight. They were also years of electoral upheaval.

Between 1933 and 1935 a half-dozen political protest movements emerged across the country. Quebec, Ontario, and
Alberta all voted out existing provincial governments in
favour of new ones. R.B. Bennett's federal Conservative government conducted a highly public inquiry into the behaviour of Canadian corporations, under the minister of trade
and commerce, Harry Stevens. Lester B. Pearson was one of
the young civil servants who worked on the resulting report.
The Stevens report exposed abuses of power, price-fixing,
profiteering, and abhorrent working conditions but resulted
in no action by Bennett. Its findings split the Conservative
caucus, Stevens resigned from cabinet, and by 1935 Bennett's
government was falling to pieces. The 1935 federal election
represented, according to one account, "the huddling together
of frightened people, uncertain of their way in the world."

It was widely understood that the Liberals were about to
retake power in the federal Parliament. Edward Young, the
incumbent Liberal member for Weyburn, was on the inves-
tigating committee of the Stevens inquiry and was the sole
member who spoke in defence of the packing houses and
retail chains that were castigated in the report. His constituents thought he had sold out to corporate interests. This
impression may have been reinforced by the private railway
car that C.L. Burton, the president of Simpson's department

stores, parked at the Weyburn station. From there Burton gave Young strategic advice during the 1935 campaign.

If the 1934 provincial campaign was conducted by the academic Reverend Douglas, who spoke as if he was giving "a course in sociology," the 1935 federal campaign for the riding of Weyburn was conducted by Tommy Douglas, the former Manitoba lightweight boxing champion. Once in the ring he was quick on his feet, tenacious, and determined to hear the bell clang in his favour in the end. During the many elections to come over his career, Douglas would always astonish his campaign managers with his level of energy. He would come out swinging and keep up the pace for fifteen rounds, exhausting his managers, organizers, and supporters with his stamina and drive. In 1935 Daniel Grant was one of Douglas's campaign advisers, and he introduced his candidate to some of the tactics of the political boxing ring. Grant was a spiritualist, a tea-leaf reader and fortune-teller, and a political nomad. He had supported the Conservatives and had been given a patronage job but was fired when the Liberals took power in Regina. Although he had no previous CCF allegiance, Grant was motivated to exact personal revenge on the Liberals and joined the Douglas campaign as organizer, chauffeur, and sometimes *agent provocateur.*

Young had recently made the mistake of saying in

Parliament that Canadians would have to settle for a "lower standard of living." Grant insisted that the statement be printed on all the Douglas campaign literature. A quick study, Douglas railed against his opponent's statement on one stage after another. Since Douglas's campaign had no budget for travel, Grant arranged campaign transportation in the form of a shiny new silver Hudson Terraplane. He persuaded the Montgomery Brothers garage to provide the vehicle on the promise of future payment and sold raffle tickets for the "Silver Bullet" at every campaign stop. Douglas averaged three campaign events a day, enrapturing the crowds with his quick wit and the CCF's people-oriented ideas, while Grant pushed enough raffle tickets to pay for the car and travel expenses. Grant urged Douglas to make his campaign lively, interesting, and appealing to common people. No stodgy lectures were allowed. If a meeting felt a little dull, Grant would stand up in the crowd and ask a provocative question.

Politics in that age was not a genteel endeavour. Fruit and rotten eggs were occasionally thrown at Douglas. The campaign car was tampered with on several occasions—in one instance all the nuts on a front wheel were loosened. Their opponents sometimes sent out young men who had been drinking to disrupt their meetings. On one occasion, in Odessa, a group of drunken toughs rushed the stage.

Douglas picked up and smashed a water jug and promised that the first person who got to him would get the sharp edge of the jug in the face. No blood was shed as the rowdies were pushed back by CCF supporters.

It was in this election that Douglas first showed himself capable of engaging in the cut and thrust of a political campaign. He was clever enough to strategize and willing to do what was necessary to win. In one case his actions almost cost him his CCF party membership. Several new parties were emerging on the prairies during these years. In August 1935 Alberta voted the Social Credit party into power for the first time. There were reports that Social Credit planned to nominate a candidate in every riding in Saskatchewan for the federal election, though in reality it did not have the resources to do this. Although there were key differences between Social Credit, which was a capitalist party, and the CCF's socialist perspective, both had populist appeal, and therefore both drew the attention of voters who were disenchanted with the mainstream parties. There was some overlap with respect to fiscal policy, and both parties emphasized increasing the purchasing power of ordinary citizens.

In an attempt to split the populist vote that was tired of both the Conservatives and the Liberals, the Liberal Party organized dummy Social Credit groups in various ridings. The idea was that even if the combined vote for the two new parties was greater than the vote for the Liberals, the Liberals might still attract more votes than either upstart individually. In Calgary, for instance, the supposed Social Credit candidate was Thomas McCaffery, a senior Liberal Party official. In Weyburn, Eric MacKay, a prominent CCF supporter and a friend of Douglas, was offered $3,500, a good annual income at the time, by Liberal organizers to run as a Social Credit candidate. He refused and told Douglas of the ploy. The candidate who eventually ran under the Social Credit banner, Morton Fletcher, was given a job in the Liberal government once they came to power in Ottawa.

Douglas decided to outflank the Liberals. His campaign also created a dummy Social Credit group whose charter members included wives of men on the CCF executive. Grant went to speak to Premier William Aberhart in Alberta, persuaded him to denounce the Liberal-sponsored Social Credit candidate as a fake and to endorse Douglas in writing. Douglas's part of the bargain was to promise that if elected as a CCF member of Parliament, he would not interfere with Social Credit provincial policies in Alberta. In this way, he walked a fine line by accepting the Social Credit endorsement, without actually being a Social Credit candidate or endorsing its policies. Understandably, the press ignored this distinction and portrayed Douglas as the CCF–Social Credit candidate. The CCF executive was furious and came close to ejecting Douglas from the party five days before the election. He argued that while he accepted Social Credit support, he did not endorse their policies except where they coincided with the CCF's. The executive was not convinced, and Douglas was saved only by his friendship with Coldwell, who threatened to resign if his friend was ejected from the party.

In later interviews Douglas would demurely imply that this and similar manoeuvres were entirely the brainchild of Dan Grant. "I said it was a dirty trick," said Douglas of the plan to have MacKay run as a fake Social Credit candidate. "[I] thanked him for calling, and would have let it go at that. But not my friend Grant.... He said, 'I'm going to talk to Aberhart.' So off he went." Although it may be true that Grant introduced Douglas to some of the stratagems of an election campaign, it would not be consistent with Douglas's intellect and independence for him to have been naively led into anything, certainly not risky political strategy. In this case, and in others in the future, he would show himself to be a capable and determined political tactician, even if he sometimes portrayed himself as above the fray.

The Liberal campaign focused on discrediting the CCF and made statements aimed at frightening farmers away from the new party. The Liberals claimed that the CCF was communist, that it would confiscate property, that it would destroy the province's economy, and that it "would tell the farmers what to do on their own farms." Douglas, who was a staunch opponent of communism and would always remain so, challenged Young to an open debate in order to refute these allegations. Young refused. In response to this refusal, Douglas and his supporters began to appear at Young's meetings, and at a well-chosen moment Douglas would walk down the aisle and challenge Young on some statement he had just made. Finally, Young agreed to a debate, which was to be his undoing.

The Douglas campaign had rented a printing plant and produced a pamphlet outlining the party's platform, which was to be distributed to all constituents. Douglas mentioned the pamphlet at several meetings, before it was sent out. Curious about its contents, Young had the local president of the Liberal Society, J.J. McCruden, a school principal, break into the printing plant one night in order to steal some copies. Douglas would later say that he was too inexperienced to think the incident was important, while Grant seized on the opportunity.

Grant laid a break-and-entry complaint with the Royal Canadian Mounted Police, demanded a search of McCruden's office, accompanied the police when they went to McCruden's school and found the stolen pamphlets, and then spread the word that the Liberals had stolen campaign material from the CCF. At the long-awaited debate between Young and Douglas, Young made a misguided attempt to downplay the issue and produced the pamphlet on stage, saying, "I don't know what all the fuss is about; there's nothing in this pamphlet, and it needn't bother anyone." Indeed, the pamphlet simply described the platform that Douglas had been campaigning on.

Douglas shot back, "There was nothing about the pamphlet I was ashamed of, but ... any man who would choose to steal my property isn't fit to be president even of the Liberal Society, let alone principal of a school, and further, any candidate who would condone such action isn't suited to represent the good people of Weyburn in the Parliament of Canada." The crowd, several thousand strong, roared its agreement. While it certainly might be the case that Grant spotted the opportunity, Douglas was quick enough on his feet to hit hard when his opponent's guard was down. On October 14, 1935, the voters of Weyburn elected Douglas to be their member of Parliament, with 44 percent of the popular vote.

On their way to Ottawa, Tommy, Irma, and Shirley stopped in Winnipeg to see Tommy's parents. His father was proud beyond words. He had always harboured the hope that his son would go far in the world, and that he might even enter politics. Even on this visit, however, his habitual reticence stopped him from expressing his great pleasure. Instead, he said, "Now, remember, laddie, the working people have put a lot of trust in you, you must never let them down." This was a directive that Douglas would follow closely and faithfully throughout his long career.

CHAPTER 5

Member of Parliament, 1935–45

Last fall there were children going to school in Saskatchewan with only gunny sacking wrapped around their feet. We have gone into homes and found mothers and children lying on piles of bedding in the corner; they did not have the proper bedding equipment or the proper clothing to meet the rigours of a very cold winter. ... What has the government of the day to offer to these people harassed from debt, needing food and clothing? ... I suggest that the time has come for action. We have a tremendous opportunity and a preponderant responsibility. The people of Canada look to us; the people of Canada trust in us; the people of Canada are counting on us; in heaven's name let us not fail them.

—FROM TOMMY DOUGLAS'S MAIDEN SPEECH IN PARLIAMENT, FEBRUARY 11, 1936

When he arrived in Ottawa, the thirty-year-old MP for Weyburn looked on Canada's capital with fresh eyes. He had never seen Parliament, though he had followed its proceedings avidly in Hansard. He knew Woodsworth and Coldwell, who were also part of the CCF caucus, but not the other party members. He was excited at the prospect of meeting the politicians whose speeches he had read. The Douglas family rented an apartment in a brick house in Centretown. They kept their home in Weyburn. Douglas expected that he would serve one term and then return to his ministry in rural Saskatchewan.

The CCF caucus in the eighteenth Parliament was tiny— it had just seven MPs—and was a close political family. Everyone had a role to play and a wide range of issues to follow. There could be no backbench complacency because there was no backbench. Even the front bench was thin. In fact, only five were "true" CCFers. Two more worked alongside for the socialist cause: Heaps, Labour MP, and Agnes Macphail of the United Farmers of Ontario. A welcome addition to that little political family, though not elected to office until 1962, was David Lewis. Lewis was a Jewish-Polish immigrant to Canada who had grown up in Montreal, had gone on to become a lawyer and a Rhodes scholar, and was a committed socialist. A formidable debater and powerful intellect, he returned from England in 1935, where he had been steeped in the Labour movement and educated by figures like John Maynard Keynes. He worked as a lawyer in Ottawa and in 1936 became the national secretary of the CCF, initially on a volunteer basis. The CCF had no research or administrative staff, except for the help of Woodsworth's daughter, Grace MacInnis. (A founding member of the CCF herself, she was married to the CCF MP Angus MacInnis. She was a CCF MLA in British Columbia and later an NDP MP.)

Woodsworth was both caucus leader and father figure. Coldwell recalled that the patriarch was informal in his conduct of caucus business. "We used to pretty much go along with what he decided." Douglas described Woodsworth as having "the complexity of a Methodist minister. Strict with his family, but not tyrannical, strict with himself, he was quite a disciplinarian, but nevertheless very kindly." Woodsworth showed Douglas how to check Hansard to ensure that he was using quotations accurately, advised him to make his maiden speech early, before he lost his nerve, and after that to not speak too often and only when certain of a position. These lessons would serve Douglas well over the years. He told Douglas, "A lot of men make speeches almost every other day, but nobody listens to them partly because they don't know what they're talking about, and partly because their material isn't well prepared."

Douglas rose to give his maiden address to the House of Commons on a cold winter day. He spoke in support of Woodsworth's resolution calling for the establishment of

Canada as a co-operative commonwealth, a society based on co-operative and socialist principles. This was a resolution with no hope of passing, but it was Woodsworth's yearly reply to the Speech from the Throne. Woodsworth had described the "present economic arrangements" as being fundamentally defective, pointing to the ongoing worldwide depression and to Canada's then-widespread unemployment as manifestations of capitalism's failure.

These planks of the CCF platform were echoed in Douglas's address. He called for the government to take action to support job creation and workers' rights, to counter corporate abuses of power such as those that had recently been outlined in the Stevens report, and to protect vulnerable Canadians. Douglas's opening words also tell us a great deal about how he saw his own role in Parliament. He said that through him, "young Canada speaks." The CCF was an outsider party whose voters sent MPs to Ottawa to work toward a new and original vision of the country. Douglas, who in photos at that time could still pass for a university student, saw himself as an advocate for a fresh vision and new ideas.

At the time of his maiden speech, Italy had just invaded Ethiopia and been condemned by the League of Nations for its aggression. Canada had imposed economic sanctions on

Italy but exempted the export of oil and nickel, both key war materials. Douglas condemned the hypocrisy of such sanctions, saying, "The modern army marches on oil. Without oil Italy could not continue to fight." He wondered why this commodity had been exempted. "Is it because the oil interests have too much influence on the powers of government?" Douglas advocated the CCF position, that Canada should establish an explicit foreign policy that promoted peace. In this same speech, he spoke of the incapacitated veterans of the First World War, who received little public support, and the similarly vulnerable population of elderly Canadians. Also, from the very start, Douglas spoke of the need for publicly funded health care. "While doctors and dentists have given of themselves until some of them are almost bankrupt," he said, "many people have had to go without the necessary dental care, the necessary medical care."

THE "YOUNG CANADA" with which Douglas identified in his maiden speech was barely surviving the Depression. Many of his generation were unable either to pursue their education or find work. They had no opportunity to get ahead. In the United States Franklin Roosevelt inspired hope with the promise of the New Deal. In Canada the Conservative government of R.B. Bennett gave no such inspiration, instead establishing labour camps where thousands of young men were paid twenty cents a day to toil on public works. This stipend did not come close to a living wage, and the camps' main achievements were to remove the unemployed from public gaze and provide a meeting place for them to organize.

In the summer of 1935 hundreds of frustrated men in the labour camps of interior British Columbia banded together and embarked on the "On to Ottawa" trek, intending to take their grievances to Parliament Hill. They travelled east in railway boxcars, and their numbers grew as they went. Roughly fourteen hundred "trekkers" arrived in Regina, where they were called "reds" and "gangsters" in the press. The Bennett government's response to this peaceful protest was to send the RCMP to keep the group from advancing east of Regina. Douglas viewed the suppression of this movement, like the crushing of the Winnipeg General Strike, as yet another demonstration that the capitalist system rebuffed common people who tried to speak out or to improve their situation in tough times. Following the 1935 election, the returning Liberal government under Mackenzie King proved to be little better than the Conservatives had been. When fifteen hundred unemployed men marched on Parliament Hill in 1937, Douglas and fellow CCF MP Grant MacNeill marched at the head of the demonstration, calling for recognition of their plight and assistance.

Of the 1930s Douglas later said, "I have always felt bitter that society allowed these young people to go without an education, and deprived some very brilliant students of an opportunity to make some real contribution. When the war broke out they took the young men and made them pilots, navigators, and tank experts at the cost of twenty-five thousand dollars each." Douglas recalled a young man in Weyburn who had the grades to go into medicine and wished to do so, but whose family had just been wiped out by crop failures and could not afford to send him to study. He had tried to help the aspiring student but was unable to raise sufficient funds. "The young man who wanted to study medicine had a very brilliant career in the air force. If we'd spent the money that made him a pilot in 1932, '33, and '34, we'd probably have had a great scientist today. As it is, we've got an insurance salesman."

In addressing the problems of the Depression, the CCF often criticized the government for acting reluctantly and without any clear plan. Thomas and Ian McLeod write that the Liberals "introduced enough reforms to avert social unrest, but not so many as to frighten the stock exchanges."

The CCF pressed the government to undertake job creation through public works, to create an unemployment insurance program, and to subsidize farm labour in order to both create work and help struggling farmers to survive. King set up a National Employment Commission and then disbanded it. Douglas and the CCF were intensely critical of the banks, which were foreclosing increasing numbers of western farms. Saskatchewan farmers were doubled over by the weight of their debts—by 1937 they owed $120 million on land estimated to be worth $100 million. Douglas repeatedly attacked the King government for its inaction.

The CCF estimated that in order to match programs that were under way south of the border, Canada should spend $5 million annually on government relief programs. In three years the Liberal government spent $2 million, enlisting its western members to argue that the CCF demands were financially unrealistic. Douglas argued that eastern Canada was taking out more from the West than it was sending back. He used figures that the Liberal cabinet minister Prof. Norman Rogers had calculated before joining the government, which showed that in 1934 the four western provinces had lost $54 million through high import tariffs, far more than they got back in federal emergency aid. The CCF proposed to spend $500 million on "work and wages" programs. Charles Dunning, the minister of finance, retorted to Douglas, "I'd like to tell my young friend that money doesn't grow on gooseberry bushes." Douglas maintained that if Canada went to war, the government would shake the bushes until it found the money. He proved to be correct. In a few short years, the government would find billions of dollars with which to prosecute the war.

IN THE PARLIAMENTARY SPEECHES of his early years, Douglas touched on a wide range of topics, both domestic and international. The ideals of his early addresses to Parliament—that the economy should be planned for public benefit rather than allowing businesses to gouge customers; that government must create a social safety net, including good public health care; and that Canada must act firmly and independently to direct its own affairs and to promote world peace— were the same themes that he espoused for the rest of his life.

Perhaps what is most remarkable about Douglas's early speeches in Parliament is that the ideals he argued for in the 1930s remained those he would champion over the next four decades. Now, at the start of the twenty-first century, we have become numbed by the inconsistencies— sometimes outright duplicity—that some political leaders demonstrate. We suspect that some politicians are motivated more by political expediency than by principle. Such are the basic ingredients for a public attitude toward politics that often vacillates between apathy and cynicism. Douglas's consistency of convictions went a long way toward explaining how he accrued widespread admiration, even from political opponents, over his long career.

As an MPP for rural Weyburn, he devoted considerable attention to farm issues, agricultural policy, and the impoverished conditions of many families in rural Saskatchewan. He challenged the government to help them. The emphasis was not on requesting handouts for farmers but rather on seeking changes on the economic playing field so that farmers had a better chance of earning a living. A guarantee, or "fixing," of wheat prices by the Bennett government had helped wheat farmers, and Douglas argued that "parity pricing" should take into account farmers' input costs so that they could be assured a profit. He appealed for crop insurance to protect farmers from droughts and other natural disasters. He decried the rampant commercial exploitation in practice at that time. Douglas earned a reputation for both well-researched arguments and memorable zingers. "Darwin said that the law of the jungle is the survival of the fittest," he told the House. "I wonder if my honourable friends think the law of economics is the survival of the slickest."

Like legions of newly elected parliamentarians of all political stripes, Douglas arrived in Ottawa full of idealistic zeal.
Of course, many of these young members soon lost their
sharp edge as the city's social functions, with their "flattery,
soft couches, and good food," wore them down. Perhaps due
in equal parts to his minister's sense of mission, the high
moral and intellectual standards set by his fellow CCF caucus
members, and his determined Scottish independence,
Douglas's crusading energy was never diminished by the
comforts of Ottawa that seduced so many young politicians.

A YEAR AFTER HE WENT TO OTTAWA, around Christmas of 1936,
Douglas received some terrible news. His father had passed
away suddenly and unexpectedly. Tom Douglas had experienced some abdominal pain but had not sought medical care.
Instead, he had stoically decided to wait at home for the pain
to pass. His appendix ruptured, and he died. When Douglas
learned that his father had been in pain but had not sought
medical attention, he was both angry and grief stricken. Why
hadn't his mother or sisters told him to see a doctor? If he
himself had been in Winnipeg, he thought, he would have
insisted on it. He fled the house in tears, then bought a ticket
to the cinema, and sat by himself to weep alone in the dark
for hours. It was the only time anyone ever saw him cry.

In his later battles for medicare, Douglas always spoke of his own childhood medical problems and of the generosity of Dr. Smith. He never mentioned his father. One cannot help speculating that he thought of his father's financial situation. Did he wonder whether things might have been different had his father not had to consider the cost of seeing the doctor?

Apart from the early tragedy of his father's untimely death, the years in Ottawa were a happy time for Tommy, Irma, and Shirley. The Douglas and Coldwell families grew close and often socialized together. An MP's salary, $4,000, was a good one at the time but not a fortune. After the Douglas family paid for their Weyburn home and their rented apartment, allowing for Tommy and Irma's habit of giving frequently and generously to churches, good causes, family and friends in need, and often paying for party expenses out of pocket, Douglas never saved much money. When he returned to Saskatchewan as premier, he carried a modest debt. CCF members were expected to donate 5 percent of their pay to the party each year, and 10 percent in election years. Douglas donated 10 percent each year, whether there was an election or not.

A keen student, Douglas listened and watched, absorbing the manners and mechanisms of Parliament, learning the ways of legislative and committee work. Committee meetings started at 11 A.M., and Parliament sat from 3 P.M. into the evening. Douglas frequently worked late in the office that he shared with Coldwell in the Centre Block. When he decided to stand for re-election and was sent to Ottawa for a second term, Shirley was of school age. Irma and Shirley stayed in Weyburn, and Irma made short visits to Ottawa to see her husband. During those years, when Parliament was in session, Douglas sometimes stayed at the YMCA or roomed with Coldwell. He didn't need fancy accommodations. Most of his waking hours were spent working, a devotion that expressed his lifelong assertion that Parliaments held the sacred trust of the people. Throughout these two terms, Douglas developed his craft as a politician and a parliamentarian.

Grace MacInnis said of Douglas's presence in the House, "He was at home right away and yet he didn't have to do silly things to show off, to be aggressive like you are when you aren't sure of yourself. Tommy was always solid. He never jumped onto a spot unless he thought it was a solid spot. He was very cautious and canny." Throughout his career, Douglas's speeches were listened to carefully, even by the opposition, just as Woodsworth's had been. Lincoln Alexander, a Progressive Conservative MP (and later lieutenant-governor of Ontario), said, "Whenever Douglas spoke, we all went, because we always learned something. He always had something to say, and something to say that was thought out." The ability of the CCF, with its tiny number of MPs, to bring about legislative change in those years depended on its members' capacity to argue intelligently and persuasively before the members of the governing party. Douglas was energized by the challenge and rose to it. In addition to his consistency of political principles, he became known for his clarity of argument and speech. Sometimes he would give lessons to Shirley on how to speak properly, saying, "Now, Shirley, you have to speak with your diaphragm," and he demonstrated speaking exercises to her saying, "Huh! Huh!" Although he was small and thin, he was able to project his voice across the House of Commons and make the CCF's position heard.

By the time he left to return to provincial politics in 1944, Douglas had a warm rapport with Prime Minister King, who had invited him to dine privately at his home on occasion. King tempted him to come over to the party in power, saying, "Tommy, you've got a brilliant career before you. I regret very much that you couldn't have found your career inside the Liberal party.... The Liberal party is broad enough to take in a lot of people who believe in progress and reform." Douglas didn't take the bait. The journalist Bruce Hutchison summed up Douglas at that time in *Maclean's* magazine: "He did not make himself popular in Parliament, but he made himself heard, and, at times, he could penetrate even the rhinoceros skin of the Government."

THROUGHOUT THE 1930s fascism's cold shadow grew steadily longer, and the slow march toward war preoccupied much of the world and Canada's Parliament. Italy invaded Ethiopia and disregarded world condemnation. With the support of Italy and Germany, General Francisco Franco led a *coup d'état* against the democratically elected government of Spain, which resulted in the Spanish Civil War. Japan invaded Manchuria, and later all of China, with brutal violence. The Nazis began their persecution of the Jews, and in 1934 murdered dissenters within their own ranks en masse.

In 1936 Douglas went to Europe as a delegate to the World Youth Congress in Geneva, made side trips to Spain where war was raging, and went to see one of Hitler's rallies in Nuremburg. Douglas was deeply disturbed to see rank upon rank of troopers saluting the führer, as German bombers roared overhead. He felt the palpable presence of evil. When he returned to Canada, he appealed for a world system of collective security to curb Nazi aggression. In the fall of 1936 he correctly predicted that without a forceful response to Hitler's Germany, Canada would ultimately be drawn into war.

The CCF condemned Hitler but also held the victorious nations of the First World War responsible for the economic hardships inflicted by the Treaty of Versailles, which allowed the rise of dictatorships. "In my opinion," said Douglas in April 1939, "it is no accident that the 'have-not' nations, Italy, Germany and Japan, are also the fascist nations." In that same speech, Douglas decried the Canadian exports of nickel to Japan that had increased fifty-fold since 1932, along with large increases in the exports of copper and iron, all key war materials. Between 1937 and 1939 the Japanese killed two and a half million Chinese civilians in what Douglas described as "a campaign of piracy in China." He equally condemned ongoing exports of war matériel to Italy, Germany, and Turkey, and said with sombre prescience, "We may be asking Canadian citizens to engage in a war in which their bodies will be lacerated and torn by the very material which is now being sent out of Canada in order to increase the dividends of certain Canadian concerns and swell the profits of United States investors. Will it be a great source of comfort to certain Canadian boys to know that the bullet which maimed them for life was made from Canadian nickel?"

As war clouds darkened, the CCF caucus was divided between Woodsworth, a lifelong pacifist, and the other caucus members who, like Douglas, believed that although war was abhorrent, there were circumstances in which the defence of free societies was obligatory. Woodsworth believed that all war was the violent outcome of capitalism, that war was always waged against the common people and therefore had to be condemned in all instances. Douglas must have thought of his own father's quandary. Tom had felt duty bound to enlist in the First World War but served in an ambulance unit rather than be obliged to kill other men.

After the German invasion of Poland in September 1939, England declared war on Germany. Mackenzie King called the Canadian Parliament to meet on September 9. At the time the Douglas family was in Saskatchewan, at their cottage on Carlyle Lake. They heard England's declaration of war on their acid-battery radio. Douglas sent Shirley scurrying to other nearby vacationers, who did not have radios, to tell them the news. Immediately, the family began packing to leave the cottage. Tommy predicted to Irma that when they returned to Weyburn the town would be empty of the unemployed men who had lined the streets since the start of the Depression. All of them would have enlisted. They returned to Weyburn so that Douglas could catch a train to return to Ottawa, and as he had predicted, they drove home through empty streets.

In Ottawa the CCF caucus deliberated their stance on the war for three emotional days. Woodsworth was steadfast in his absolutely pacifist views. Douglas and the other caucus members took the same position as most MPs—that Hitler's fascism had to be confronted by force and that the debate in Parliament should focus on Canada's role in opposing the Nazis.

Douglas and Woodsworth had long discussions on the subject. Douglas pointed out that Woodsworth had spent most of his life building up trade unions, all of whose slow gains were being wiped out overnight by fascism in Germany. Woodsworth would not budge. Douglas did not take this issue lightly. He had read the works of Gandhi and other pacifist writers, but he had also seen the Nazi troops in Nuremburg and met priests who carried machine guns to fight Franco in Spain. He could not support a philosophy of absolute pacifism, for sometimes it was necessary to use force to protect civilized society. He later said, "I have responsibilities to defend my child, my home, and my wife, to protect my community and the weaker members of society. I can't abrogate this merely on the philosophical idea that force is never correct … if you accept the completely absolutist position of the pacifist, then you are saying that you are prepared to allow someone else who has no such scruples to destroy all the values you've built up." He reached a painful conclusion: "I recognized then that if you came to a choice between losing freedom of speech, religion, association, thought, and all the things that make life worth living, and resorting to force, you'd use force."

With the CCF leader and its caucus unable to reach an agreement, Woodsworth handed in his resignation as leader, which the caucus ignored. Even in disagreement, the CCF would not abandon their leader. As Grant MacNeill recalled, "We were sorry about J.S.'s position on the war. We were in agony on the whole thing. There was no ill feeling. We just loved him, felt we should protect him, but we couldn't go along with him." Finally, it was agreed that Woodsworth would speak only for himself in the House debate, and Coldwell would speak for the party. The position of the party on the war was to advocate that there be no overseas commitments of Canadians at that time, only defensive military measures, that civil liberties must be protected in Canada, and that plans must be made for the postwar period.

Woodsworth had suffered a stroke, and when he rose to speak in the House of Commons, he could not see properly and was partly paralyzed on one side. Douglas sat next to him and handed him his cue cards, with a few words on each card in large block letters. In an unusual gesture that demonstrated the great respect with which Woodsworth was regarded, Prime Minister King rose to say a few words before Woodsworth's speech. He indicated that he expected Woodsworth to take a position contrary to most of the House, and warned the House that he also expected its members to listen and to say nothing unkind, for Woodsworth had been the conscience of Parliament for a quarter of a century. Despite this admonishment, Woodsworth's address opposing the declaration of war by Canada was marred by a few catcalls and jeers. After he sat down, Coldwell spoke for the party, and in this way a tacit transfer of leadership occurred. Douglas himself was torn between his loyalty to Woodsworth and his view of the war. He said later, "With Woodsworth, you put your political principle first and political consequences second ... and I think the CCF survived only because of Woodsworth's unyielding attitude. Compromise wasn't part of his make-up."

As Canada's manufacturing industry geared up to meet the demands of the war machine, Douglas and Coldwell proposed that the Defence Production Act include an amendment to limit manufacturers' profits on arms to 5 percent. The minister of munitions and supply, C.D. Howe, accepted the amendment, but the manufacturers did not, and the amendment was removed by order-in-council. Douglas was scandalized, saying, "The arms manufacturers actually went on strike. If the workers, or the soldiers, had taken such a position, think of the outcry."

When another federal election was called in March 1940, Douglas again put his name forward. A major assertion in the CCF platform was that if there was to be conscription of men for the war, there should also be conscription of wealth. The party advocated for equality of sacrifice. Douglas was returned to Parliament. Meanwhile, he enlisted with the Second Battalion of the South Saskatchewan regiment. When Parliament was not in session, he drilled and trained, rising from corporal to lieutenant and then to the rank of captain. In 1941 the Winnipeg Grenadiers were looking for men to go overseas, and Douglas volunteered. There was no hesitation on account of his young family: like many men of the time he saw military service as his duty. He was prevented from going to Hong Kong with the Grenadiers only on account of his leg condition. The Grenadiers, minimally trained and poorly equipped, joined the British garrison in Hong Kong in October 1941. They were raw recruits and totally unequipped to meet the Japanese attack, which came shortly thereafter. The British and Canadians surrendered on

Christmas Day. Douglas had many personal friends in Hong Kong who were either killed or captured by the Japanese.

Two major themes animated CCF criticism of Canadian policy during the war: the first had to do with the use of Canadian troops, and the second with the use of Canadian wealth. The CCF was always mindful that Canadian troops should be independently deployed under Canadian control. Both in Hong Kong and later in the 1942 raid on Dieppe, Douglas and the CCF charged that Canadian troops were sacrificed on British initiative. The inadequately trained and supplied troops had been sent to Hong Kong on the strength of a British Military Intelligence assessment that said a Japanese attack was unlikely. At Dieppe, mostly Canadian troops were landed on a well-defended beach, despite the fact that an air and naval bombardment intended to destroy the German defensive positions was called off by British command. A third of the men who were landed at Dieppe died. The raid was a bloody fiasco. King defended the British War Office, as he always did, and Douglas asked whether Canadian military command was losing control of its own troops. In matters of foreign and military policy, he believed that despite being closely allied with two of the world's greatest powers—Britain and later the United States—it was crucial for Canada to direct its own affairs.

On domestic wartime affairs, Douglas spoke publicly against the internment of Japanese Canadians and encountered vitriolic racism both inside and outside the CCF.

The economic prosperity that the war brought with it could not be denied, but the CCF contended that companies should not make excessive profits while men gave their lives to the cause. Questionable military procurements came under CCF attack, for example, when a lucrative Bren gun contract went to a small firm without being tendered and appeared to be based on patronage. The party never gained any political traction with its assertion that wealth should be conscripted for war along with men. Throughout the war the CCF struck a precarious balance, supporting the war effort while criticizing aspects of its conduct. This stance forced the CCF to answer criticism from all sides. The right questioned their patriotism when they criticized government actions, and the pacifists in their ranks felt betrayed when they supported the government at all.

Toward the end of the war, as it became clear that the Allies would prevail, Douglas and the CCF looked to the postwar years. The decades after the First World War had seen the feverish prosperity of the 1920s give way to the Depression of the 1930s, which the CCF, as well as economists like John Maynard Keynes, viewed to be the predictable outcome of capitalism operating without government regulation. In Europe the punishing conditions that the Versailles treaty had imposed on Germany set the stage for Hitler's rise. Douglas sharply protested the signing of the Teheran and Yalta agreements. He saw them as a repetition of the Versailles treaty's mistakes—that the world and the spoils of war were divided among the victors without proper consideration of the desires of nations and peoples who would be affected. "I took the position that the great powers had no right to sit down and divide the world like a pie."

The pressing question asked by the CCF at home in Canada was what would be done for returning soldiers. They worried about what would drive the economy as war production halted and hundreds of thousands of young men returned in need of a job and a future. Douglas exhorted Parliament to remember Canada's great debt to its soldiers. He worried that if demobilized veterans did not find work, confrontations like the Winnipeg General Strike would be replayed. In 1945, toward the end of the war, he went to Europe and spent three months visiting Saskatchewan troops. During this trip he fell and reinjured his leg. The injury would flare up from time to time for the rest of his life. He met men who had been unemployed prior to enlistment and had marched behind him on Parliament Hill with Grant MacNeill. He met farm boys who had heard him speak at rallies in Saskatchewan. He found that many of the soldiers, knowing that victory was imminent, had begun to worry about their prospects in peace.

CHAPTER 6

A New Premier, 1940–45

> It was a fairly rough campaign because the Liberals had by
> this time begun to smell defeat in the air. Their attacks
> became almost frenzied. We had now ceased to become
> Communists, which we had been called in previous elec-
> tions, because the Communists had become respectable....
> We, who for years had opposed Hitler when other people
> were saying he wasn't a bad fellow, were now classified as
> National Socialists. They made wild assertions that we
> were going to take farms, confiscate businesses, and drive
> all the industries out of the province. The attacks became
> more hysterical with every passing day.
> —TOMMY DOUGLAS, 1958, ON THE 1944 SASKATCHEWAN
> ELECTION

Tommy Douglas, and indeed the early CCF movement,
always held humanity firmly at the core of their political
beliefs and motivations. Their dream was a society in which
people were as free as possible to pursue individual self-
realization, while working co-operatively in order that all
could live a "dignified, and a rich and varied life." Douglas
said of the CCF, "This is more than a political movement ...
it is a people's movement, a movement of men and women

who have dedicated their lives to making the brotherhood of man a living reality."

What would such a society look like, and what role would government have in it? Over the late 1930s and early '40s, at study groups and conferences addressing issues of law, economic theory, industrial development, and social programs, some specific concepts crystallized and were artic-ulated by the CCF. One consistent thread that ran through their discussions was that human self-realization and dignity did not exist in an abstract realm but rather were dependent on, and only possible in, an environment of economic opportunity and security, social security, and democratic freedoms. Another consistent idea in these discussions was that government should have a role in both ensuring demo-cratic freedoms and creating the tangible systems of eco-nomic and social well-being. Although in modern Canadian society this role of government has become both accepted and expected to a large degree, they were radical ideas at the time of the CCF's birth.

One could observe that there was an area of overlap of the goals of the CCF and those espousing economic libertarian-ism, which was the status quo in Canada at the time. Both advocated for the societal and economic conditions in which they believed that individuals could develop most fully and richly. The profound difference was that the libertarian believed that the best condition for human development was one of unrestricted capitalistic competition, while the CCF believed that individuals could be most free in an environment of societal co-operation. For the libertarian, economic profit was the measuring stick of a healthy society. The CCF contended that though a vibrant economy was a highly desirable and crucial part of a healthy society, it should not be considered an end in itself. Instead, an economy should be oriented toward meeting human needs before profits, and some of the generated wealth should help to build a humanitarian society.

The CCF felt that government should occupy a planning role in the economy and sometimes take an ownership position. Certain key sectors such as finance and utilities, which tended to become monopolies and were essential to the functioning of the broad economy, should be carefully regulated, or in some cases owned outright by the public. The economy should be a mix of private, public, and co-operative activity. Social security should be achieved through publicly funded health care, education, and welfare services. People's individual rights to organize in their workplaces, and to voice their opinions freely, should be protected in law. An average person should be able to pursue study, work, recreation, artistic endeavours, and business opportunities as he or she might see fit. Underpinning the CCF position was always, as Al Johnson, one of Canada's pre-eminent and most creative public servants, writes in *Dream No Little Dreams: A Biography of the Douglas Government of Saskatchewan, 1944–61*, "a passionate belief in the common man: in his ability and his right to govern himself; his right to the dignity and self-assurance to which all men are born; and his right to the kind of economic and social security which the CCF believed to be essential to self-realization."

THE EARLY 1940s were heady years for the CCF. Despite a tiny presence in the federal Parliament, the party's national popularity grew rapidly. CCF members vocally supported the interests of everyday Canadians, who began to look forward to the end of the war and tried to imagine what kind of country theirs could become. They wanted to hear a postwar plan, and the CCF articulated one. The CCF argued that after the war there should be a new era of proactive governmental economic planning for the good of all citizens. David Lewis wrote that people believed "if the resources of our country can be organized effectively for war, they can and shall be organized for abundance and security when peace comes. This is the reason for the tremendous growth of the

CCF at the present time." Gallup polls showed that the CCF's support nationally rose from 10 percent in January 1942, to 21 percent in September 1943, to 29 percent in September 1944, at which time it was one percentage point ahead of both the Liberals and Conservatives.

Since the mid-1930s the CCF's ideas had struck a popular chord in western Canada, particularly in Saskatchewan. Unfortunately, the Saskatchewan provincial organization had become increasingly fractious. George Williams, the party's leader and president, had worked to silence Woodsworth and other pacifists, and suppressed dissenting opinions within his own party to such an extent that he had been accused of behaving like a dictator. "I quote President Roosevelt," he declared defiantly. "Be loyal to the party or withdraw." Williams was not very good at finding consensus or building the kind of grassroots support that the CCF needed. His bullying ways clashed with Coldwell's more democratic approach. Coldwell wrote of Williams, "He is without doubt the most cunning individual with whom it has ever been my misfortune to be associated.... I have made up my mind that I will be no party to placing George H. Williams in the Premier's chair." In 1940 Coldwell began to urge Douglas to turn his efforts to provincial politics. He also began to press the Saskatchewan CCF to separate the functions of provincial leader and party president, and he spread the word that Douglas would make a fine party president. Williams had always insisted that the two roles were indivisible.

Just prior to leaving to serve in Europe with the Canadian Light Horse, Williams wrote a long, rambling letter to the CCF executive, complaining bitterly that Coldwell coveted his job and that Douglas was working to undermine him. He was half right: Coldwell was working to undermine him and wanted his close friend and ally, Douglas, to take his place. As when Dan Grant had manoeuvred on his behalf with Aberhart, however, Douglas managed to keep a discreet distance between himself and the jockeying until 1941, when he contested the Saskatchewan CCF presidency. Williams ran in absentia from his post in England. Douglas won, and Clarence Fines became the new vice-president. The party paper, the *Commonwealth,* and Fines both declared that, just as Williams had always asserted, the two CCF offices of party leadership and presidency were one and the same and Douglas occupied both. Now, however, Williams's supporters argued that the positions were separate, and it was agreed that the party would be leaderless until a special convention could be organized and the question settled once and for all. In 1942 Douglas was elected leader, the delegates voted to split the leadership and party presidency, and Clarence Fines was elected president.

When asked years later about the friction of that time, Douglas replied mildly, "There's always been a coolness between Mr. Coldwell and Mr. Williams." Douglas was always honest, but not always entirely frank. Unfailingly, he told the kind half of every story. With a few exceptions, Douglas had complimentary words even for bitter political opponents and broadly generous assessments of members of his own staff, even when they demonstrated incompetence. (This happened rarely because Douglas was good at choosing people, and he drove them hard.) Thus, the intensely personal struggle between Coldwell and Williams became "a coolness" in Douglas's account.

After the fighting was done, he quickly invited Williams loyalists into his inner circle and later offered Williams his choice of cabinet post. It became very characteristic of Douglas that following the resolution of conflicts within his own party, he would pull out all stops to heal wounds and bring the losers into the winners' camp. Three decades later in 1970, when Allan Blakeney and Roy Romanow contested the Saskatchewan NDP leadership and Blakeney prevailed, Douglas was on stage next to Romanow as delegates applauded the new leader. Even as Douglas and

Romanow stood clapping, Douglas was already saying to Romanow over the din, "Now, Roy, every orchestra needs a conductor, and lots of good fiddlers. You just keep up the fiddling, and one day you will be holding the baton." In 1971, when Blakeney became premier, he made Romanow deputy premier. Romanow himself assumed the top position in 1991.

Tommy Douglas—Baptist minister, parliamentarian, and new leader of the Saskatchewan CCF—and Clarence Fines—school teacher, Regina alderman, and party president—set out to win Saskatchewan for the CCF. They mounted a fundraising campaign, a membership drive, and set up a network of committees to study issues and prepare the CCF for power. The network was headed by a planning committee, which was presided over by Douglas and Fines and included both war supporters and pacifists. It was as the new leader of the Saskatchewan CCF that Douglas began to demonstrate his great gift for unifying and inspiring people. His flair for organization and delegation was as important as the ideas he championed, and Saskatchewan was fertile ground for ground-up political organization. Blakeney described it as a province where if some kind of need arose in the community, "The normal reaction in rural Saskatchewan at that time was 'let's call a meeting.'"

Meanwhile, the Liberal government in Saskatchewan led by W.J. Patterson was due to hold an election no later than June 1943. Patterson knew his party was in trouble, however, and in April of that year passed a bill to prolong his government's life by one year, citing the exigencies of war. Still sitting in the House of Commons, Douglas pressed King to disallow the bill, pointing out that "the moment that a people are governed without their consent, we have moved from Democracy into Fascism." King responded that he was opposed to parliaments extending their own terms of office. Privately, he chastised the premier, but he took no action.

If anything, the delay ultimately helped the CCF by giving the party an additional year to organize and cement its growing popularity. Between 1941 and 1944 the number of dues-paying party members grew from five thousand to twenty-six thousand. The big-business support that the Liberals enjoyed was not available to the CCF, but in its place they built an active, enthusiastic grassroots organization funded by individuals. With a strong tradition in direct democracy, the Saskatchewan CCF had a long-standing practice of holding an annual convention where all party policies were presented, debated, and voted on. Delegates from all provincial electoral districts were organized into panels and committees to consider specific issues. From

1942 to 1944 the topics covered grew in scope and increased in detail, to include provincial budgeting, program planning, education, social services, labour legislation, housing, natural resources development, agriculture, models of public ownership, and health care. Douglas and Fines also established new committees to deal with party finances, radio broadcasting, and educational literature. Notably, the study of issues by these committees was not primarily directed at criticizing the governing party but rather was a constructive exercise aimed at developing a comprehensive election platform and preparing the CCF to lead.

At a national conference in Regina before the 1944 election, Douglas and the CCF consolidated their platform. The result, "Program for Saskatchewan," was not simply a platform to win an election, it was a plan to reinvent a province. First, it prioritized economic growth through resource and industrial development, as a necessity for prosperity and in order to fund new social programs. Second, the platform set out detailed plans for new or reformed programs in health, education, and social services. Third, it articulated in some detail the reforms to an antiquated public service that would be necessary to achieve these goals. The national CCF knew there was a good chance of a victory in Saskatchewan and believed it to be of crucial importance that this CCF government be successful in order to pave the way for victories elsewhere. As leader, organizer, and frequently as mentor to his fellow CCFers, Douglas was deeply engaged in the task of shaping the policies.

When the 1944 campaign got under way, the CCF and its leader were well prepared. The party held "winter schools" in Regina and Saskatoon to inspire and educate their candidates, campaign managers, and organizers. They printed the main points of the CCF's program on a small card that organizers and canvassers carried with them. The platform included farm security legislation, labour rights, support of the co-operative movement, improvements to public schools, public investment in industry, and a promise to work toward a system of publicly funded health care. The platform said nothing of the principles of socialism and made no mention at all of political theory. This was not an effort at concealment. It was simply decided that the campaign platform should explain practical issues in terms that were relevant to people's lives and make promises that were achievable. This was to be Douglas's style of campaigning and political priority-setting throughout the rest of his career: while the ethos was socialist, he distilled from it a limited number of understandable, achievable goals that had a direct relevance to people's lives.

THE LIBERALS RAN a negative campaign, sometimes denouncing the CCF as Nazis, on other occasions as Bolsheviks, and charging that the CCF would confiscate farms and cancel insurance policies. Liberal MPP Hubert Staines declared that the CCF "fails to conform to its Hitlerite prototype only in its lack of the swastika and the goosestep." The Liberal Party issued a statement saying, "There has emerged out of the Coldwell fog the true character of national socialism, its statism and its sameness with Communism." This can only be judged as a somewhat confused accusation, since it seems to equate the CCF with both fascism and communism in the same sentence. The Liberals, hoping to inspire fear among both God- and beer-loving voters, warned that the CCF would close both churches and beer parlours. All the major city newspapers supported the Liberals despite their adoption of possibly the most unconvincing campaign slogan ever used in Canadian politics: "Please Give Us Another Chance!"

The mood of the CCF campaign was ebullient. Douglas attended picnics in the afternoons and rallies in the evenings. He drove from meeting to meeting and wrote scripts for his radio broadcasts in his hotel at night. "Those who were there are sure they will never again experience anything quite like Douglas in the 1944 campaign," wrote Doris Shackleton in her 1975 biography of him, remembering those days. "His presence, his electric vitality and the sheer eloquence of his voice as he set out to win Saskatchewan were scarcely more remarkable than the open joy of the people who heard him."

The Douglas family spent a lot of time together on the political trail. Shirley's earliest memory of her childhood is of a political rally, watching her father come out on stage into the light, and seeing hundreds of hands reach out to him, clapping for him. He would invariably begin with a joke, and as he moved into the substance of the speech, she would be mesmerized by his words, along with the crowd. Often, "Uncle Charlie," Charlie Broughton, organized these events. He was a transplanted Englishman with a charming manner, and he travelled with his fiddle. Charlie and Irma would go ahead, because they made up the advance party and were also the warm-up act, with Charlie on fiddle and Irma on piano. Douglas and Shirley would follow a little later. Saskatchewan roads were generally unpaved at the time and sometimes very muddy. It was not unusual for their car to get mired in the mud at some point, and Douglas would trudge off to the nearest farm to seek the help of a farmer with a horse and team. Of Shirley, Douglas would tell people, "She's stuck to me like a burr." A rally could last well into the middle of the night. Irma was a quietly formidable campaigner. She was well versed in the language and lore of popular sports, including hockey and curling, and by making the rounds at these meetings she would both win over voters and gather useful intelligence.

Corporate Canada watched the election with grave concern. A committee was formed that included the presidents of Noranda Mines, Imperial Oil, International Nickel, and Massey-Harris, to coordinate opposition to the CCF campaign. Simpson's offered its catalogue network to distribute Liberal literature, and mainstream newspapers in Saskatchewan carried headlines such as "Socialism Leads to Dictatorship," "All Opposition Banned if CCF Wins Power," "CCF Government Would Take Away Farms," and "Would You Like to Pay 20% Tax on Everything?" No such measures had ever been proposed by the CCF. On the eve of the election, the Regina *Leader-Post* warned that the election of the CCF "would affect vitally the way of living of every individual, will affect the right to own and use property ... [and] start Canada on the road to strife and devastation that has been followed by European countries."

In contrast to such frightening and baseless imputations, Douglas promised a new society. He offered voters a choice between conditions "as they were before the war: a period of free enterprise and all the poverty it caused, or a change to a commonwealth of social justice." Saskatchewan was a province of farmers who for decades had been gouged by high import tariffs and price-fixing. They had seen thousands of farms repossessed and their livelihoods and dreams swept away like the soil on their drought-stricken fields. They had suffered these indignities without any meaningful government assistance. They had lived through a time that was awful enough in its real challenges that they were not easily spooked by corporate scaremongers. It was the vision of Douglas and the CCF that resonated. The 1944 campaign was remarkable not only as a demonstration of Douglas's charisma and socialism's popular appeal at that time but also as an example of democracy in action. Ordinary people worked to put their vision of government into power, despite massive efforts by big business to preserve the status quo.

One night Douglas spoke to a packed room at Regina City Hall. As he often did, he told a story. It was his now-legendary Parable of the White Cats and the Black Cats. Several generations of CCF and NDP politicians have faithfully retold it, but it was Douglas's story first. "Every four years in Mouseland, which was a democratic country, the mice held an election," he told his audience. "One year they would elect the black cats. And conditions—for mice—were terrible. So after four years they rose up in protest, threw out the black cats, and—elected the white cats. The white cats preyed on the mice even more terribly than their predecessors had. So next time—back in went the black ones. Until one day, a small mouse stood up in his corner and said, 'Let us elect mice.' They called him a radical, a Communist, a National Socialist. But the idea spread. Mice got the message. The day came …"

As it did for the mice in the parable, the CCF's day came. On election night Shirley darted in and out of the campaign headquarters and asked Irma and the volunteer workers repeatedly, "Is my father the premier yet?" By ten o'clock they were able to answer that he was. Broughton lifted Shirley onto the stage and announced that she would say a few words. A bright ten-year-old, she proclaimed in the language that she had heard from the adults around her, "Your shackles have been broken!" Douglas was hoisted onto the shoulders of his supporters and carried through the streets of Weyburn in a spontaneous parade.

When the returns had all been counted, the CCF held forty-seven of the fifty-two seats in the Saskatchewan legislature. Opposed by some of the largest, most powerful business interests in the country, with all the established newspapers aligned against them, a party that had never before been in power achieved a landslide electoral victory. A party of idealists and social activists, preachers, and working people had set out to reinvent the province of Saskatchewan. They would eventually make an indelible impression on Canada's political landscape.

FOLLOWING THE ELECTION Douglas and Fines retreated to the Douglas family cottage at Carlyle Lake for several days, in order to plan the cabinet and the government. On July 10, 1944, Lieutenant-Governor Archibald McNab swore in Canada's first socialist administration. Douglas announced in the legislature that three new departments were to be created: the department of social welfare, the department of co-operatives, and the department of labour. He also proposed that the pay of a cabinet minister be reduced from $7,000 to $5,000 so that the creation of the new departments would not result in increased spending on ministers' salaries. Douglas's view was, and always remained, that a people's government had to be careful with the people's money.

Douglas gave Williams his choice of portfolio, and he chose agriculture, though he passed away soon after. Fines became the provincial treasurer. Thirty-one-year-old Woodrow Lloyd, a school principal, was made minister of education. John Wesley Corman, former mayor of Moose Jaw and the only lawyer in the caucus, became the attorney general. He was a former Liberal who had a signature line that he used at the end of his radio addresses: "You are born into the old parties. You have to think your way into the CCF. Good night." Douglas himself took the health port-folio, as the reform of the health-care system was central to his concerns.

Eleanor McKinnon, the daughter of a noted Liberal at Calvary Baptist Church, was one of Douglas's most impor-tant new staff members. At Irma's suggestion, Douglas hired her away from her job as the secretary to the superintendent of the Weyburn Mental Hospital. Irma must have been con-vinced that her professional experience would equip her to run a premier's office. With one interruption in service, she would be the centre of calm in a perpetual whirlwind as Douglas's secretary for the next forty-two years. McKinnon dealt with foreign dignitaries and irate constituents with equal aplomb. On one occasion, when an angry man appeared with a gun saying that he was going to kill the pre-mier, she deftly indicated that Douglas was in another office, when in fact he was in the adjacent cabinet room. McKinnon called security, and then when Douglas returned from the meeting and learned what had happened, restrained him from going after the would-be assassin.

The set of challenges that faced Douglas was formidable.

He was an experienced parliamentarian but had never been part of a ruling party. Much of his caucus had never sat in a legislature, and his ministers had no experience running government departments. Having been completely left out of the wartime manufacturing boom that had benefited some provinces, Saskatchewan had a significant debt that had been weighing it down since the Depression. Corporations and media were hostile, as was the federal government. Meanwhile, some who read too creatively into the Book of Revelations warned that the advent of this government signalled the impending arrival of Armageddon. Others charged that Russians had taken over Saskatchewan and were beaming lethal rays at its citizens.

To make matters yet more difficult, the CCF arrived in the former government's offices to find that many file cabinets had been emptied. Thousands of files had been destroyed, including all departmental correspondence in the premier's office. Some of the files that remained were sufficiently incriminating to make one wonder about the contents of the others that disappeared. One document contained instructions to land agents on what threats to use to intimidate farmers who were suspected of being CCF sympathizers. Another outlined a scam involving the purple dye used to colour tax-free gasoline for agriculture. A company purchased the dye from a supplier, marked it up with a generous profit, and sold it to the provincial government. The problem was that the company didn't exist.

In these early months Douglas's office was the scene of barely contained chaos, besieged by well-wishers, complainers, cranks, and new government employees. The CCF had its share of people with idealistic but impractical schemes, which had to be quietly shelved. Douglas operated his office with an "open door, no appointments" policy, and relied on McKinnon to maintain order. In the midst of this frenzy Douglas took sustenance when he could. He began his career as premier on a steady diet of raisin pie and coffee. In time his ulcer rejected this regimen, and he switched to milk and poached eggs.

The provincial Liberals fully expected that the CCF would have one gloriously failed term in office and then disappear. It could have happened. It would have been easy for them to get it all wrong, and few predicted that they would hold power in Saskatchewan continuously for the next two decades. While there were forces working against the party, it also had much in its favour. The CCF had a commanding majority in the provincial legislature, and owed no favours to anyone except the people of Saskatchewan. An enthusiastic public, many of whom had little formal education but were self-taught and well informed, were eager for new ideas and as farmers and small-business people, had their feet very much on the ground. As Blakeney put it, "He (Douglas) got a chance in Saskatchewan to work with people who believed that change was possible. That was the big thing about Saskatchewan: the number of cynics per thousand people was lower than anywhere else in Canada.... These people could take an idea, and run with it, and make it work because they were hugely practical." Also heavily on the assets side of the ledger, the CCF had Douglas— indomitable, idealistic, hard-nosed, and capable of arousing the best instincts in those around him through a mixture of humour and high expectations.

In a special session of the legislature, between October 19 and November 10, 1944, the new government began to put its platform into law by passing 76 bills. Within eighteen months, it had passed a staggering 196 pieces of legislation. These addressed many rural issues, including crop-failure insurance, protections from farm foreclosure, the creation of co-operative farms for war veterans, larger school units, and rural electrification. It began offering certain publicly funded health-care services and raised mothers' allowances by 20 percent. Among the provincial government's new laws were many innovations that we now take for granted in Canada, such as the right of public-service workers to unionize, a legal basis for collective bargaining, and holiday pay for workers. The foundation for large-scale reform of government was laid with the creation of a government purchasing agency, a bill to allow the government to enter the auto and fire insurance business, and an economic advisory board.

By the end of 1944 Douglas's government had stabilized the farm debt crisis, and begun a program of economic planning and resource development. Early in 1945 the Saskatchewan Government Insurance Office came into being as a commercial venture. It would prove to be both popularly subscribed and profitable. Saskatchewan issued new bonds to develop provincial resources, which were bought mostly by ordinary citizens. Even though rumours spread among investment dealers that the province would default, the offering was oversubscribed by 30 percent.

Two major themes emerged from the flurry of legislative activity. First, many of the new initiatives were guided by the CCF's belief that for people to truly have the freedom to develop themselves, society must provide them with a minimum of economic and social security and legal protection of democratic rights and freedoms. Second, this was an administration which understood that the economy and government needed to generate wealth if society was to prosper and the government was to provide services.

At the legislature, an expectation of hard work and mutual trust grew from the premier's example. Douglas's cabinets have been described as Quaker in style, in that the premier often tried to avoid an actual vote and instead sought the "sense of the meeting" to arrive at consensus. He directed the discussion in a Socratic manner by asking questions and soliciting the opinions of his ministers. He had a knack for getting to the crux of an issue, making it seem obvious. The McLeods write, "He could take complex issues and reduce them to vivid populist imagery." At lunch he lined up in the legislature cafeteria with everyone else, sat with civil servants and backbenchers, and thus heard from all levels.

To be in Douglas's cabinet, however collegial, was never easy. Blakeney recalled, "Yesterday was the desired time to deliver whatever he was asking for. People forgave him because he worked that way himself all the time." A relentless worker, he drove himself and his staff to the brink of exhaustion. It was at this time that his temper began to show itself. In public Douglas was endlessly supportive of his staff, full of praise, and always diplomatic. In private he could be a model of openness and fairness in considering conflicting ideas. However, his colleagues knew that he could also deliver a stinging rebuke, not usually for disagreement but for the ultimate transgression—not getting one's work done. Three members of cabinet, including Douglas, soon suffered from ulcers. Eleanor McKinnon brought three half-pints of milk with straws to each cabinet meeting in order to soothe the ailing.

On one occasion, two members of cabinet visited Irma. They pleaded with her to intercede on their behalf. "Please say something to him," they said. "We're exhausted, and working as hard as we possibly can, but it doesn't satisfy him." Irma responded helplessly, "I can't do anything about it. He's pushing himself just as hard." There was nothing else to say. They knew that Irma was right. Douglas worked so hard that his cabinet also worried about his health. They bought him a reclining lounge chair so that he could put his bad leg up. Once, they all pitched in to send him on a cruise in order for him (and likely themselves) to have a much-needed break.

As premier, Douglas did not entertain at home. He seemed to realize that now that he was in power, he could no longer enjoy the kind of close, personal socializing that had been part of his life in Ottawa. He needed to preserve his home for his family. He remained compassionate at a personal level, and Blakeney recalls Douglas's taking him under his wing as a religious minister would, when his young wife passed away.

Irma defended the house as an oasis of calm. She had the telephone company install a cut-off switch on the side of the phone. When the front door opened and Douglas came home for dinner, she tripped the cut-off switch, and he would have at least a brief respite. He went to the legislature early in the morning, came home for dinner, napped, and then went back to work in the evening. If things were going well, the family chatted over dinner. If he was preoccupied, he ate silently.

An adopted daughter, Joan, joined the family in the spring of 1946. While her husband carried a heavy load as premier, Irma took on herself all the household responsibilities of paying the bills, arranging repairs, and clothing and caring for the children. Irma was also Tommy's second set of eyes and ears. She was fun and easy to get along with and easily entered Regina's political circles. There, she never said a negative word to anyone, but appraised people carefully. She would warn Tommy if she thought someone was untrustworthy or out to obtain some kind of personal advantage, and he would seek her advice on especially challenging problems. Those who knew the couple observed that Irma was every bit a match to Tommy in determination and intellect, and that they had a very equal and close marriage.

Only when Douglas came back late in the evening was it possible to salvage some family time. If it was still early enough, they might go for a walk. Shirley remembered that on these occasions it was "as if a wall came down" between her father and the family. Such moments were treasured, for otherwise Douglas drove himself at full tilt from the moment he awoke until the moment he went to bed. Sometimes, late at night, Douglas would put on the radio broadcast of fights from Madison Square Garden, strip to his undershirt, and shadow-box in the dark.

CHAPTER 7

The CCF in Power, 1945–60

> The newspapers said we were going to socialize everything, that the government would own the farms, the corner store, the barber-shop, and the beauty parlour, and that everybody would be working for the state. When that didn't happen, they had to give some explanation. So the explanation was that we had betrayed our principles, we were no longer Socialists, we were reactionaries and had departed from our original ideas. In effect, we were now traitors, because we didn't do the horrible things they promised we would. They had built up a straw man and now they were knocking it down.
> —TOMMY DOUGLAS, 1958, ON THE CCF GOVERNMENT IN SASKATCHEWAN

One December day Tommy and Irma were putting up the Christmas tree. Shirley, who was then a teenager, was out shopping at Simpson's. She arrived home distraught and said, "Somebody stole my wallet." Perhaps she expected her parents to be upset or her father to pick up the phone and call the police. He was the premier, after all.

Tommy asked Shirley, "And what did you do about it?"

"I went to the floorwalker," she said. That would be the salesperson, in modern vernacular.

"The floorwalker? What would you do that for?" said Tommy. "Why did you go to the floorwalker? He can't get your wallet back."

"What should I have done?" asked Shirley.

"You should have gone after the man who took your wallet! Where was he?"

Irma intervened at this point, with a stern look and a single utterance. "Tommy," she said. After all, Shirley was young. But the premier did not pick up the phone and call the police. He couldn't understand why his daughter hadn't chased the thief herself, which is what Douglas would have done. He wasn't just talking tough. Decades later, when he was in his seventies, he and Irma were accosted by a thief while on holiday in Jamaica, and Douglas chased him down an alley.

In 1945 the electorate of Saskatchewan did not get a timid socialist theorist for a premier. Indeed, it was not because the voters were socialists that they had elected a socialist government. Rather, Saskatchewan supported the CCF because the party and its leader proposed practical measures with tangible benefits. Voters continued to elect them election after election, because they delivered what they had promised. "How socialist was the CCF government of Saskatchewan?" asks Doris Shackleton rhetorically. She then writes, "Anyone answering will begin, 'It depends on what you mean.'"

If one considers the government's balance sheet, it was not the work of people whose wallets bled as freely as their hearts. Douglas's government was financially cautious, even conservative. Previous governments had run deficits and accrued so much debt that Saskatchewan had the second highest per capita debt of any province in Canada when the CCF took office. From this starting point the Douglas government recorded a budget surplus in each of its seventeen years and steadily paid down the debt accrued by its predecessors. Despite the dire predictions made by business naysayers, no bonds were defaulted, public works were funded on a pay-as-you-go basis, and new services were phased in incrementally as they became affordable.

It was fortunately coincident that the postwar years were boom years for the North American economy. Even so, Douglas's government was more fiscally responsible than any in the memory of Saskatchewan residents, and much more socially progressive than other, wealthier Canadian provinces. It actively sought investors and developers to do business in the province and encouraged major growth in the development of natural resources such as oil and potash. As well, it ensured that a greater share of the wealth derived from burgeoning resource development flowed into public coffers in the form of royalties and taxes. This money was then spent on further economic and infrastructure projects as well as on social services. The CCF government was active and adept in attracting industry to the province. Their modus operandi was that if the government wanted to deliver services, it had to have revenue from economic activity, which required good infrastructure and a favourable business environment.

If one considers the CCF government's record on supporting the vulnerable, defending civil rights, giving farm and labour interests a legitimate voice, providing better services, and building a fairer society, then the CCF was socialist to the core. What Douglas's government put into practice was not some kind of theoretical or doctrinaire socialism. Like the architect who builds the most interesting structure when constrained by an unusual building site, the Douglas government inherited tight finances and an underdeveloped province and pushed itself to provide creative, sensible, and uniquely Canadian solutions to the practical problems faced by a poor region. It advanced its dual goals of economic and social development, and thus demonstrated that the all too frequent rhetoric that each of these two goals must come at the expense of the other is simply not true. The principle that guided the Douglas government in Saskatchewan was that economic and social development should encourage each other, and they did.

His attitude toward provincial finances came in part from his working-class background. He once described his own father, saying, "He was the kind of man that would owe no one, with the exception of buying our house, of course, which we had to buy by paying so much a month. That was foreign to him. But he never in his life bought anything on credit. That was his pride, that he owed no one any money." As a youth, Douglas worked at odd jobs to help support his family, and paid his own way through the course of his religious education. He also shared the rural culture of Saskatchewan, which, along with an active co-op movement, was an economy of small entrepreneurs. Each farmer's hope was to raise a good crop, sell it at a profit, and one day save enough to own his or her own piece of land, free and clear. Douglas understood both the frugality and the independent spirit of the people of Saskatchewan, and the new CCF government was formed in this mould.

The other driver of the Douglas government's prudence was their awareness that they could not count on the province's ability to borrow money from private sources. At one point the head of the Regina office of a major brokerage firm asked Clarence Fines if he would personally buy Saskatchewan bonds, whose soundness was being questioned in the media. Fines replied that he certainly would. To prove it, he borrowed $15,000 and used it to buy $5,000 in bonds from each of three major brokerages at ninety-two cents on the dollar. The word spread that the provincial treasurer was buying provincial bonds, the bond prices rose, and the Saskatchewan government was able to continue to issue bonds when it needed to. Two years later, Fines, who was a canny investor as well as a CCFer, sold his bonds at a tidy profit. Then he was accused by the Liberal opposition of taking advantage of his position as provincial treasurer. He retorted that the members of the opposition were free to do as he had done and buy provincial bonds.

Douglas anticipated correctly that his government would receive no financial favours from Ottawa. In fact, the federal government tried to cripple his administration early on by suddenly calling in a multi-million-dollar loan that had been made available to destitute farmers for seed purchases under the provincial Liberal governments. When the CCF passed legislation that taxed Canadian Pacific and other companies' vast undeveloped mineral rights, and enacted bills that gave farmers certain protections from foreclosures, the rail and mortgage corporations appealed to the federal government to disallow the legislation by means of an obscure provision of the British North America Act. Initially, Ottawa seemed to be willing to comply with these requests.

Douglas took to the radio. He appealed to the people of Saskatchewan to write to Ottawa to express their outrage at the federal government's threatened interference with his mineral rights taxes and farm protections. Listeners could have imagined him jabbing his index finger in the air in trademark fashion as he said,

> Let me here issue a word of warning to those who are moving heaven and earth to have this legislation disallowed. I want to tell them that they are not dealing in this case with a government of tired old men who are merely holding on to power for the spoils of office with a hope of finding a final resting place in the Senate. They are dealing with a government fresh from the people with a mandate to carry out the people's wishes. Those wishes will be carried out. If these vested interests succeed in persuading the federal government to disallow this legislation we still have other resources at our

disposal and we will not hesitate to use them. We
were elected to protect the homes and the security
of our people and we will use every legitimate
method which we possess to attain that end.

Douglas exhorted listeners to write their federal representatives. Letters poured in to Ottawa, and under this pressure
the panel of federal ministers tasked with considering disal-
lowance of the provincial legislation retreated. Douglas's five
successive election victories in Saskatchewan were greatly
helped by his government's aligning itself squarely with the
province's people, and fighting for their interests. No one
was going to pick the pocket of Saskatchewan without
Premier Tommy Douglas and Treasurer Clarence Fines chas-
ing them down.

The counterpoint to Douglas's sometimes testy relations
with Ottawa was that he believed a strong central government was necessary for a planned economy and nationwide
equality of services. He urged the federal government to
move forward on social service and health initiatives in the
same manner that he was pressing ahead with them in
Saskatchewan, and to share the costs. On issues such as
unemployment insurance and pensions, it was clear that
Saskatchewan did not have the financial means to back a

comprehensive plan. At federal–provincial conferences, Douglas called for greater involvement by the federal government in this and similar programs, usually encountered a lack of interest, and went home to do what was achievable in Saskatchewan.

The central governments that Douglas dealt with, including those led by Mackenzie King, frequently talked about social programs in their election platforms but usually failed to follow through once they were elected. The Dominion Provincial Conference on Reconstruction of 1945 produced a Green Book that laid out plans for national health insurance, a planned economy, and a social safety net. Douglas praised it effusively, but though it helped the Liberals in the following federal election, he would later lament it as a lost opportunity, for its recommendations were not to be implemented nationally for decades.

Oddly to some, one of the three photos that hung in Premier Douglas's office was a portrait of Mackenzie King. The others were of Woodsworth and Abraham Lincoln. The allegiance to J.S. Woodsworth was obvious, less so the others. Of Lincoln, Douglas once said that the aim of the CCF was to free people from economic slavery, as Lincoln had freed the American slaves. Douglas was repeatedly disappointed by King's failure to deliver on his electoral promises, but the two had a warm personal relationship. It might be a stretch to say they were intimates, but King invited Douglas over for dinner on several occasions as a young MP. After Douglas became premier and was visiting King in Ottawa, the prime minister once kept him up late and confided in him the devious strategies he had used to manipulate his own cabinet on the issue of wartime conscription. King once told Douglas that he reminded him of his deceased brother, and Douglas always said that King had been very kind to him when he was a young parliamentarian. For Douglas, underlying sentiment meant a great deal in spite of party politics.

A CENTRAL OPERATIONAL FEATURE of the CCF's provincial government was that it and the civil service took a new, proactive role in the planning of economic development and social services. They had some great successes and made a few mistakes. The latter were mostly due to excessive enthusiasm, and the fact that planning and oversight mechanisms were still being developed within a government that was creating new roles for itself.

A healthy share of the government's early blunders were the work of Joe Phelps, who, as minister of natural resources in Douglas's first cabinet, soon put his ministry in charge of a range of enterprises, including the processing of timber, fish, fur, wood, hides, and clay. His vision ran ahead of prudence, and often his actions preceded cabinet assent. When his colleagues asked him to slow down and consult them, he once said, "Never say whoa in the middle of a puddle!" Most of these ventures did create jobs, especially in the northern part of the province where they were badly needed in primarily First Nations communities. They also lost money. In the growing family of Saskatchewan Crown corporations, these ventures accounted for only about 5 percent of government investment in industry, and profits of other Crown corporations greatly overshadowed their losses. Nonetheless, the losses provided fodder that critics would use for decades to argue that government had no place in business.

The Economic Advisory Committee inherited from the previous government made it clear that they were not planners, so Douglas and his cabinet went looking for the right experts to help plan a mixed socialist economy. The premier was never shy of seeking the most qualified people for the best possible advice, and when he found them he gave them a great deal of latitude.

David Lewis suggested that Douglas invite George Cadbury to advise them. Cadbury was the scion of the confectionary dynasty of the same name. The Cadbury company had been founded in the United Kingdom in the early nineteenth century by a prosperous Quaker family that took an active interest in the well-being of their workers. Their historical interest in operating a successful business while promoting social justice had been passed down through the generations along with the Cadbury name. George Cadbury had worked in food processing, had directed British wartime aircraft production for three years, was closely involved with the British Labour Party, and was a committed socialist. By mid-1945 Douglas was courting him to come to Saskatchewan.

On January 1, 1946, Cadbury assumed a dual role as chairman of the Economic Advisory and Planning Board, in which he would be dedicated to economic planning, and as chief industrial executive, charged with bringing sound management to the Crown corporations. Cadbury's two agencies reported directly to cabinet and were central to making the government of Saskatchewan into an efficient, rational, and professional organization. He worked closely with Douglas and Fines, and though his rank was a step below cabinet minister, some ministers felt that he had a higher status than they did.

A tall man of formidable intellect, Cadbury spoke persuasively in meetings and also knew how to manoeuvre quietly in the civil service. Douglas gave him a broad mandate to apply his business approach to the government's problems. At the first of the cabinet Planning Board meetings, Cadbury argued for restraint in social spending until the government invested more money to increase the productivity of the economy. He reinforced the CCF tenet that nationalization for the sake of nationalization was unwise, and that government should invest in business only where there was a clear public interest to do so. He insisted on feasibility studies and full cabinet discussions prior to the establishment of any government-run enterprise. Rather than cry whoa in the middle of a puddle, he did his best to keep the government out of them. Cadbury completely reorganized the existing Crown corporations to make them accountable and oriented to the government's goals.

Under his watchful eye, the government rejected proposals to invest in breweries, coal mines, and oil exploration. Saskatchewan already owned the telephone system and the provincial liquor stores when Douglas became premier. It proceeded to create a province-wide bus service. It gave Saskatchewan Power a monopoly on natural gas distribution and directed it to buy up small electricity producers throughout the province to build what would eventually become a state-owned, province-wide power grid. In these new initiatives, a social agenda was blended with an economic one. For instance, bus lines and utilities in remote locales would tend to be money-losers whether undertaken by private or public industry. A business run only for profit would not operate them. However, the province could choose to make such services available everywhere by using the profits from more heavily populated urban areas to compensate for rural operating losses. Thus, there was a social reason to own these businesses.

Douglas was determined to improve life for rural residents, and from 1949 onward the government brought electricity to forty thousand farms. This program did more than any other to bring the living standard on farms closer to that in cities. When flying over Saskatchewan, Douglas used to love looking down at the twinkle of rural electric lights. In net terms, the Crown utilities and most of their businesses were profitable. (René Lévesque may have noticed Saskatchewan's success: when he became minister of natural resources in Quebec in 1961, he soon directed Hydro-Québec to buy and if necessary expropriate all of that province's regional power suppliers.)

Clarence Fines, provincial treasurer, was central to the Douglas government's success. He was the de facto deputy premier, devoting his attention to the inner workings of government and budget control. Fines balanced the budget every year. He squeezed money out of every corner, just as he had once scrounged to pay for Coldwell's radio broadcasts. He was to many an enigma, for as one contemporary put it, he was "a dedicated socialist with the acumen of a tycoon."

Douglas and Fines were very much a governing partnership. Douglas was the visionary while Fines watched the balance sheet, but rather than conflicting, they complemented each other. Blakeney, who was in cabinet late in the Douglas government's years, speculated that Douglas and Fines sometimes decided on a yes-man, no-man act in advance. "They did what struck me as a little dog and pony show, where ... I am sure it was arranged in advance," said Blakeney. On some new proposed spending, Fines would declare it unaffordable, and Tommy would disagree, bluster, and finally insist that they had to find a way to afford it. The supposed conflict between Douglas and Fines would evaporate as quickly as it had arisen, and Blakeney explained, "the routine was that Tommy would overrule Clarence at a few given intervals so that the other cabinet ministers, of whom I was one, would not think that this was all being decided by the people in finance, but that we had something to say about how this government was going forward. It was a very good operation, and it was a nice piece of cabinet psychology, because it's hard to get cabinet ministers to accept the proposition that the world as they see it from their ministry is not quite the same as it is from the centre."

On many other occasions Douglas would gush enthusiastically at a minister's proposal. Then he would turn to Fines, who would declare that it was a budgetary impossibility, and Douglas would sigh in disappointment at this unfortunate constraint, while still having been able to support the initiative in spirit. Douglas's cabinets may have been open and collegial, but with Fines's help, he had ways of directing affairs. Al Johnson recalled one way in which the understanding between the two men worked. When Fines needed Douglas's intervention in a Treasury Board review that had become deadlocked, for example, Fines would give Johnson a private signal to fetch the premier. Douglas then would "drop in" on the meeting and, invariably, make a "suggestion" that had the effect of backing up Fines. Fines won himself and the CCF the respect of business, and reassured moderate voters that the party governed wisely. He often reined in party activists and his fellow cabinet members when they proposed costly government programs or wished to embark on them too soon.

In his position of quiet power, Fines was unafraid to occasionally attend to problems personally. Marian Anderson, the great African-American contralto and a courageous pioneer among artists of colour, visited Regina in 1956. Fines was at the Saskatchewan Hotel to meet her. Seeing her, the front desk staff informed Anderson that there were no rooms at the hotel. Famously, she had in 1939 been barred from performing at the Daughters of the American Revolution's Constitution Hall in Washington, D.C. In response, President Franklin Roosevelt and his wife, Eleanor, arranged for Anderson to sing before seventy-five thousand people at the Lincoln Memorial on Easter Sunday of the same year. Fines was not about to see her turned away from a hotel in Regina. He asked to speak to the hotel manager. He inquired whether they had a liquor licence. They did. He indicated that if they wished to keep it, a room should be found for Anderson—who was soon a guest at the hotel.

IN 1948 A NEW PUBLIC SERVICE ACT effected radical changes to the civil service. These included a merit system for recruitment and promotion, clear job descriptions that linked duties and responsibilities to rates of pay, and hiring reforms to eliminate patronage. Eventually, ambitious and well-organized recruitment programs, offering innovations such as funded educational leaves in return for service commitments, were implemented to attract the best young talent.

Douglas was determined to hire people based on skill rather than political stripe. He regularly found himself faced with senior CCF party officials who believed that he should appoint only party members to senior civil service positions. This, after all, had been the long-standing practice of previous governments. Douglas shot back on one occasion, "It is easier to make a CCFer out of an engineer than it is to make an engineer out of a CCFer."

He set out to energize the civil service and make it a forward-looking, merit-based institution. The new government hired and developed young, ambitious people like Allan Blakeney and Roy Romanow, who would both later become premiers of the province; Al Johnson, who would rise to be a senior public servant in both provincial and federal governments and a president of the CBC; Tommy Shoyama, a Japanese-Canadian economist who later became deputy minister of finance in Pierre Trudeau's government; and Art Wakabayashi, who would become an assistant deputy minister in Ottawa. Of note, the hiring of Japanese Canadians elicited openly racist criticism both from outside and inside the CCF, and Douglas lambasted the critics.

One of the premier's great strengths was his ability to encourage dynamic professionals to take the government's goals as their own and then allow them the freedom to do their best work. As one senior civil servant later said, "It was this sense of tremendous freedom that made the Saskatchewan public service so attractive to those of us that worked there." Douglas often spoke of planning as being essential to socialism, and worked to build institutions that would outlast the four-year political tenure of elected officials. He hoped for a government structure that fostered forward-thinkers, that stood apart from the rough and tumble of partisan politics, and that had a mandate to apply the latest scientific, social, and economic theories to the work of government.

For example, agricultural advisers were charged with bringing the best, most advanced scientific farming practices to Saskatchewan. Researchers learned that turning over the soil the traditional way caused erosion, but that this could be minimized by planting instead in the stubble left by the previous year's crop. Once, when a group of farming experts visited from Russia, Douglas proudly showed off a field where the new technique had been employed. One of the Russians said, with a restrained grin, "The man from Georgia," meaning Stalin, "likes to look across the fields and see the soil all turned over. He likes the soil to be dark."

Douglas said, "Well, we all do because it looks very nice, but it's very bad agriculture."

The Russian replied carefully, "I'm not sure if the man from Georgia would understand that."

Douglas had no time for this, and found it ridiculous. While Russian Communists, to whom the CCF had been compared both maliciously and inaccurately, had descended into Stalin's dark and fearful totalitarian state, Saskatchewan was open and forward-looking, quite willing to dispense with traditions when modern knowledge showed a better way.

When Douglas first arrived in the premier's office, provincial budgeting had been a static, rudimentary exercise. Many departments simply reprinted their budgets from the previous year. This habit would no longer be possible with the flurry of new programs and initiatives, and a new government that wanted to reconfigure its civil service machinery. Early in his efforts to assist Douglas to establish a framework for the many ongoing changes, Cadbury's board articulated the practical objectives of government, then ranked them in order of importance. In September 1946 the order was firstly resource and agricultural development, then transportation and communication, followed by education and preventive health, industrial and utility development, curative health, social welfare, labour policies, and finally physical and cultural amenities and community planning. Using this framework, the board evaluated the province's expenditures according to the degree that they advanced the agreed-on goals. All departments were required to submit a three-part "work program" to justify their budget proposals. In this way budgeting became an explicit and critical policy exercise, targeted at both scrutinizing the effectiveness of specific areas of spending, and planning to advance broad goals.

A new system emerged in which boards and agencies were given a great deal of autonomy and yet remained answerable to the cabinet and legislature. This allowed individual initiative to be channelled within a broader vision and proved very effective. Highly qualified people went to work in Saskatchewan in order to be part of a socialist movement and also to be part of a creative and invigorating civil service. Its strength did not go unnoticed. In 1964, after a Liberal provincial election victory was followed by the firing of a host of well-regarded bureaucrats, so many of them were hired into top positions by the Liberal federal government that they became known in Ottawa as the Saskatchewan Mafia.

As a whole, the new premier, the people who surrounded him, and their innovations in civil service management had the effect of changing the provincial government of Saskatchewan from a largely reactionary institution into one that addressed questions of enduring importance for all modern governments: *What do we want to achieve for our citizens? What's the best way to achieve it? Are we getting value for money?*

THE DOUGLAS GOVERNMENT affected Saskatchewan daily life in diverse ways. The CCF was as interested in rights and democracy as it was in economic planning. It gave labour new rights and gave civil servants the right to organize. One of the great legislative advances of the government was the passage in 1947 of the Saskatchewan Bill of Rights. It protected freedom of conscience, opinion, religion, expression, and association. It prohibited arbitrary arrest and detention. It also prohibited discrimination in employment, property ownership, accommodation and services, and in professional associations and unions. It preceded the United Nations' adoption of the Universal Declaration of Human Rights by a year and came a full thirteen years before the Canadian Bill of Rights, which was enacted in 1960. Even prior to the end of the Second World War, the CCF invited Japanese-Canadian internees to resettle in Saskatchewan, at a time when most parts of Canada were trying to keep Japanese Canadians from settling among them.

One aspect of the socialist program that never grew as robustly as Douglas wished was the co-op movement. In 1949 he became minister of co-operation and co-operative development. He dreamed of an economy in which workers had a stake in the businesses they laboured in and benefited from their success while supporting their fellows. The co-op movement grew during the CCF tenure until membership exceeded half a million. Still, Saskatchewan's co-ops occupied a cautious middle ground in the economy rather than redefining the relationship between primary producers and the business interests that profited from them, as Douglas had hoped. Experiments at establishing farming co-operatives became international showpieces, but they did not endure. The most successful co-ops may have been those set up in the north to manage fur and fish commerce. The self-help ethos of the co-ops found a good fit within the culture of the First Nations peoples. In most other locales, however, co-operators lacked the fervour that Douglas and other CCFers held for the concept. Although committed socialists usually supported co-ops, co-op members were not necessarily socialists. For many, being part of a co-op was just the best economic option available at a particular time and could be put aside in favour of a better option later.

The Douglas government had similarly mixed results with First Nations issues. These properly fell into federal jurisdiction, but this circumstance did not prevent Douglas from having a warm rapport with Dan Kennedy, an

Assiniboine chief. Nor did it keep him from being disturbed by the low quality of education and health care on many reserves, and by the discrimination encountered by First Nations war veterans. Since the provincial government did not have jurisdiction, Douglas tried to help using the tools he knew best, by promoting organization. He and his legal adviser, Morris Shumiatcher, facilitated the creation of the Union of Saskatchewan Indians in 1946, which could present a united front to federal bureaucrats. Officials in Ottawa became annoyed with the provincial involvement, especially with Shumiatcher. After a while, the First Nations also began to feel that Shumiatcher was setting the agenda at their meetings and complained to Douglas about it. Shumiatcher withdrew and soon left public service. Over the years that followed, a time in which many First Nations and Métis migrated from the reserves to Saskatchewan's cities, no level of government could claim that it meaningfully addressed the problems of persistent racism, unemployment, and poverty that these groups faced.

The CCF did succeed in enhancing the cultural life of its constituents. The Saskatchewan Arts Board, created in 1948, became the first institution of its kind in North America. It promoted the visual arts, music, literature, and handicrafts, and presided over the development of a generation of musicians, writers, and artists. Douglas believed that the people of the prairies were hungry for artistic and intellectual stimulation. He never gave up the fundamental idea that he was in the premier's chair to improve people's lives, not simply their economic output.

Douglas maintained that he was doing God's work. He described the rise of unions and co-operatives in the nineteenth century as "an attempt to apply in the realm of economics the teaching of all the great religions." He once said, "When we devote our time and energy to the building of the co-operative movement, we are doing more than working for ourselves; we are helping mankind along a road that leads to social justice and economic emancipation." Yet somewhere along the line Douglas stopped going to church. It was not that he lost his faith. He stayed on the roster of Baptist ministers, still guest-preached from time to time when invited to do so, and quoted scripture as part of his regular way of speech. Perhaps it was because as premier he could not commune closely with God in the public setting of a church. His voters would be sure to surround him and ply him with political questions after the service. In keeping with his mother's instincts, Douglas had allowed his Christian faith to guide him into a life of public service. Having done that, he returned to a spiritual practice more like his father's, a private relationship between himself and his God.

By the end of the 1950s, after fifteen years of CCF government, Saskatchewan residents had higher incomes, electricity on farms, paved roads, and a more secure and enjoyable life. From 1956 to 1960 electrical generating capacity doubled, as did the value of resource production. By 1960 work had started on a $200 million Saskatchewan River dam, seventy-two senior citizens' homes were under construction, and Saskatchewan had the most advanced public-health-care programs in the country.

One great irony of the CCF's success was that the comforts brought by their remarkable achievements perhaps diminished the public's thirst for idealism. The Douglas government became known for putting practical, people-oriented legislation and competent delivery of public services to the fore. In any event, many good CCFers would have argued that such virtues were a core part of socialism—real socialism, not a demonized propaganda version. As years of good government continued uninterrupted, some party purists murmured nonetheless that in the public eye, Douglas's integrity and sound leadership shone more brightly than the traditional CCF rallying cries for greater social and economic justice. Lewie Lloyd, brother of

Woodrow Lloyd, the education minister, wrote to Douglas, "… the old spirit is dead, we have some good ministers but say what you like I doubt if we could win an election without Tommy Douglas." The party, wrote Douglas in reply, would have to learn to operate differently as the world changed.

THE DOUGLAS GIRLS grew up during their father's tenure in Regina. Shirley decided to pursue a career in acting and took a part-time job at a department store. Joan chose to become a nurse. Irma managed the household affairs, including buying her husband's clothes for him. Always impeccably dressed, he would sometimes look down as if surprised by a shirt or tie and remark that it was rather nice. He advised his daughters that "you can be as radical as you like, but you must dress like a banker."

The family discovered the W.K. Chop Suey House on South Railway Avenue, where they went to sit in a booth and eat dinner every Sunday evening. Tommy ate more here than he ever did elsewhere, and Irma was delighted. Somehow, the steaming Chinese dishes did not bother his ulcer. The Douglas family would maintain a friendship with the restaurateurs, the Yee family, for the rest of their lives. When Tommy and Irma later travelled to China, Irma reported that the food in China was fine, but "not as good as the W.K."

Douglas read voraciously but never took up any of the hobbies that middle-aged men often indulge in. He once told a biographer that she would find him to be a very boring person, because all he ever did was work. His doctor recommended that he take up a pastime. He tried fishing and couldn't stand it. He had no interest in golf. Douglas and Fines once started a mink farm together as both a hobby and business venture, but after discovering that they had tried to breed two minks of the same sex and realizing that they had no natural ability as mink farmers, they sold it. They invested together in a drive-in movie theatre, and the press had a field day with the notion that Douglas, a Baptist minister, was a co-owner in what they dubbed the "Premier's Passion Pit." His main recreation was daily walks. When he was travelling by train, he was legendary for getting off at every station and walking briskly up and down the platform, dragging his colleagues with him. When airplane travel became the norm, he did the same on flight stopovers, marching back and forth between gates.

The cottage at Carlyle Lake was the family's refuge. There Douglas would lie in the sun reading in the morning, and then go through a ritual of donning his bathing cap, splashing water on his neck, then his arms, and go for a swim. He favoured the side-stroke. He would go for long swims so that, before he turned back, only the faraway dot of his bathing cap could be seen from the shore. Then he would swim back, the family would have lunch, and Tommy and Irma would go for a walk and collect the mail.

In Regina, whenever he had free time, Douglas went to the hospital to visit patients. He also spent time in hospital for his leg. His osteomyelitis had started to act up again, ever since he had reinjured his leg in Europe in 1945. He had to be admitted to hospital for treatment almost yearly, and he would dutifully alternate between the public hospital and the Catholic hospital in Regina so there would be no hint of favouritism. Each year, despite the worries of his staff, he was discharged and returned to the business of running Saskatchewan.

CHAPTER 8

Universal Health Care, 1944–62

> To me it seems to be sheer nonsense to suggest that med-
> ical care is something which ought to be measured just in
> dollars. When we're talking about medical care we're talk-
> ing about our sense of values. Do we think human life is
> important? Do we think that the best medical care which
> is available is something to which people are entitled, by
> virtue of belonging to a civilized community? … I believe
> that the great bulk of the people of this province support
> the idea of the medical care plan. I believe they will
> indicate they are willing to pay for it, providing the cost
> is spread equitably on the basis of ability to pay. The
> only ones who are likely to oppose it are those who fear
> that they will have to help those less fortunate than
> themselves …
>
> —TOMMY DOUGLAS, IN THE SASKATCHEWAN LEGISLATURE,
> OCTOBER 13, 1961

When Douglas stood in the Saskatchewan legislature in
1961 and made the case for full medicare, he said, "I lay in
a children's hospital in Winnipeg on and off for three years.
My parents couldn't afford the services of an outstanding
surgeon. I had my leg hacked and cut again and again,

without any success. The only reason I can walk today, Mr. Speaker, is because a doctor doing charity work, one of the great bone surgeons of Winnipeg, who was later killed in the First World War, came into that hospital one day with a group of students, took an interest in my case, and took it over."

Perhaps Douglas did not feel shy about bringing his personal experiences into political debate because he understood that political decisions impact the lives of people. He did not fight for universal health care for some abstract, theoretical reason. He fought for it because he knew the helplessness of being a poor immigrant boy whose parents had no money to pay for the specialized treatment he needed. No one, thought Douglas, should be placed in that position. From this experience grew his belief that in a civilized society all people should have the medical care they require, irrespective of their wealth and ability to pay.

Shirley Douglas recalled that when she was a small girl, during her father's first term in Ottawa, she fell ill with a fever. She was hospitalized and was soon diagnosed with measles. With care, it would pass, the family was told. Shirley was impressed by the nurses' starched white uniforms and caps and recalls the hospital as a rather lovely place. Outside her window was a playground. Her father came to see her and declared immediately that he was taking her home. The staff asked him why, and he said that he didn't want his daughter to be lying in a hospital bed and listening to the children playing outside. At great expense Douglas hired private nurses to attend to Shirley around the clock at home. She was surprised because she had been quite pleased with the hospital. She came to understand that her father had a clear, painful memory from his own boyhood of lying sick in bed and listening to the other children playing outside. It had been such a terrible experience that he could not bear to see his daughter go through anything resembling it.

To most Canadians, it has become a core part of our national ethos that health care should be equally available to all regardless of ability to pay. It seems intuitively to be fair and right. The corollary is that we accept a collective responsibility to fund this service with our tax dollars. When we worry that we may lack a national identity, we sometimes pay universal health care a backhanded compliment by grousing that this, of all things, is the one feature of our nation that is almost universally supported. Perhaps we feel a little embarrassed that a social service has become a defining aspect of our collective psyche. We should not sell this notion short. Although there are certainly other ideas and institutions that we could strengthen as part of our national identity, our belief in universal health care constitutes a strong statement about our nation's values. The notion that all Canadians should have access to high-quality health care on an equal basis is an assertion that all human lives have equal value, and that a civilized nation should be collectively concerned for the health and welfare of its citizens.

The CCF did not invent the idea of a public-health-care system. The National Health Service was created in Britain in 1948 under a Labour government, and several other industrialized countries implemented publicly funded health care in the years after the Second World War. In Canada, such a program had been a well-used plank in Liberal federal election platforms since the early years of the twentieth century, though one that was never followed by action.

What the CCF, and Douglas in particular, can rightly take credit for is the commitment and political will to make universal health care a reality in Canada. For the first half of the century, Canada's health care operated in a free-market system identical to that of our southern neighbours. At the time of this writing, the United States still has the dubious distinction of being the only industrialized country in the world that does not have a public-health-care system for the general population. There only the elderly and destitute have access to a public system, while the heart-rending legislative efforts of President Barack Obama's Democrats have succeeded only in legislating reforms to the private insurance industry. Not coincidentally, the United States has a significantly more expensive system that produces markedly worse health outcomes when compared with the rest of the industrialized world and even with some developing nations. Without Douglas and the CCF, it is likely that Canada would now have a health-care system identical to that of the United States.

The Liberals promised universal health insurance in 1919 but once elected took no action. They campaigned on it in 1945 but never delivered. Despite being in office in the prosperous interval between 1921 and 1930, and again from 1935 to 1957, the Liberals' only advance after three decades of power was to pass a national Hospital Insurance Act. This act contained what Douglas called a "joker" because it promised federal support for hospital insurance provided that at least Ontario or Quebec as well as four other provinces entered into it. Predictably, given the fractious state of federal–provincial politics, this consensus never emerged. Ontario wanted to let private business deal with it, and Quebec wished to go their own way. Some themes endure in Canadian politics.

In 1961 Douglas and his CCF government, having already made huge advances in socialized hospital care in Saskatchewan, staked all their political capital on a push to bring full universal health insurance, or medicare, to Saskatchewan. They fought for it tooth and nail and soon proved that it could be done successfully. Their example worked so well that other provinces and the federal government could not help taking notice and eventually following suit. However, the struggle to bring medicare into existence was one of the most bitter fights of Tommy Douglas's political career. It was also the accomplishment that he was most proud of. Through this achievement, Douglas has touched the life of every Canadian who visits a doctor or walks through the doors of a hospital.

FOLLOWING THE CCF's first election victory in 1944, Douglas brought Dr. Henry Sigerist, a professor of social and preventive medicine at Johns Hopkins University in Baltimore, to Saskatchewan to advise the province on reforming the health-care system. By bringing to bear his usual mix of frugality and charm, Douglas persuaded Sigerist to come out of medical duty, without pay, and covered only his expenses. Sigerist stayed for just a month—he was on his way to a public-health post in India—but in that month, he travelled widely to hear presentations and assess conditions in the province. He remarked to Douglas that given the state of the outhouses in rural Saskatchewan, he was surprised that the citizens of the province did not suffer from chronic constipation. Nonetheless, the recommendations he produced initiated the CCF's development of the health-care system, a process that was to continue over the next two decades. The CCF's infrastructure improvements and the arrival of flush toilets would also make the ceremonial burning of the outhouse a rural Saskatchewan ritual over the ensuing years.

Sigerist noted that the province was near bankruptcy and cautioned it to proceed gradually as finances allowed. He advised the government to begin to build the groundwork and facilities that would allow it to offer progressively more public services. Before full hospital insurance could be implemented, he observed, more hospitals had to be built first. At that time Saskatchewan had the fewest hospital beds per capita in Canada. The ultimate goal should be kept in mind, said Sigerist: "to provide complete medical services to all the people of the Province, irrespective of their economic status, and irrespective of whether they live in town or country."

In 1944 the CCF started by addressing the needs of the most vulnerable groups of patients, instituting programs to fund all cancer, psychiatric, and venereal disease treatment. On Sigerist's advice, Douglas set up the Health Services Planning Commission to oversee new programs. A husband-and-wife team, Dr. Mindel Sheps and Dr. Cecil Sheps, came from Winnipeg to head the commission. Early in 1945 government-funded medical care was also extended to the elderly, the blind, recipients of mothers' allowances, and wards of the state. In Swift Current, "Health Region No. 1," a pilot project of full medicare, was established. It included then-innovative public-health measures such as water-safety testing and routine immunization. It worked well, proving on a small scale that such a program was doable, despite the Saskatchewan College of Physicians and Surgeons' attempts to dissuade the doctors of Swift Current from participating.

As the province's finances stabilized, the government renovated or built thirty-three hospitals. In the spring of 1946 Douglas promised that there would be province-wide hospital insurance running by January 1, 1947. His own Planning Commission felt this was too rapid a pace, but he insisted on pushing ahead. On Sigerist's recommendation, Douglas hired Dr. Fred Mott, the deputy surgeon general of the United States, and Dr. Len Rosenfeld, another American expert in public health, to join the Planning Commission and assist with the implementation of the program. They came to Saskatchewan, assessed the situation, and agreed that it couldn't be done on the premier's timeline.

In most areas Douglas heeded his expert advisers when they recommended cautious, slow progress. In the field of health he sometimes insisted on moving forward despite advice to the contrary. Stubbornly, Douglas told the Planning Commission that they would either bring in the plan by January 1 or be replaced by people who could. Meanwhile, murmurs of opposition by hospital administrators began to bubble up. In December the entire executive of the Saskatchewan Hospital Association arrived in Douglas's office to tell him that they would not co-operate with his plans. They pointed out that many of the hospitals had been built by church funds, charitable donations, and community money and could not simply be taken over.

Douglas explained that the province would not be taking over ownership or administration of the hospitals. It would just pay their bills. His legislation centralized financing, not administration. The advantage, in an era when between 30 and 60 percent of hospital bills went unpaid, was obvious. Despite all obstacles, the hospital plan began on time, and proved successful and popular. The hospitals became ardent supporters of the provincial plan, and within seven years

Saskatchewan had the most hospital beds per capita in Canada.

For the next decade the costs of the Saskatchewan hospital-insurance program made it prohibitive to take the next step toward full public coverage of medical care. In 1947, for instance, hospital insurance consumed 15 percent of the provincial budget, and this figure rose to 20 percent by 1955. The program derived about a fifth of its funding from a 1 percent increase in sales taxes, about two-fifths from a small per capita tax, and two-fifths from general revenues—which effectively were derived from royalties received in the resources sector. In the meantime, the other provinces sent staff to Regina to examine the Saskatchewan plan, and soon British Columbia, Alberta, and Nova Scotia set up similar plans. All of this served to create a national demand for hospital insurance, and eventually, in 1957, the Progressive Conservative government of John Diefenbaker passed the Hospital Insurance and Diagnostic Services Act, which would see Ottawa paying about half of the cost of any provincially run hospital insurance, without stipulating that Ontario or Quebec must participate as the Liberal legislation had required. Practically speaking, any province that did *not* participate in public hospital insurance was subsidizing the hospital care of other provinces while receiving no benefit itself. This situation created a powerful incentive for each province to participate. By 1961 all had signed on. The same leverage would later be used to encourage all provinces to undertake full medicare, but not until Douglas and the CCF proved that such a system could work in Canada by making it a reality in Saskatchewan.

Throughout the 1950s Douglas promised repeatedly that his own government would introduce a medicare program once it could afford to do so. On an almost annual basis Douglas asked that Ottawa consider contributing to a pilot program for full medicare in Saskatchewan. There was little interest. At a planning conference in April 1959, with the province's balance sheet healthier than ever, cabinet decided that the time had come to proceed with province-wide universal health insurance. The program of full medicare was to be, it was hoped, a profound expression of the party's values, a landmark achievement for Saskatchewan, and, ideally, an example that could be followed throughout the country.

At first, the Saskatchewan College of Physicians and Surgeons expressed a wish for consultation rather than their outright opposition. In November the cabinet laid out the framework for the plan, and on December 16, 1959, Douglas announced in a radio broadcast that Saskatchewan would proceed with medicare. The five principles articulated were that the plan would be prepaid on an insurance basis rather than by the patient at the time of care, that coverage would be universal, of high quality, publicly administered, and acceptable both to patients and health-care workers. The premier concluded by announcing the government's intention to create the Advisory Planning Committee on Medical Care with equal representation by government, the public, and the medical profession. Acknowledging that there were already murmurs of apprehension in the medical community, Douglas said, "We have no intention of shoving some pre-conceived plan down doctors' throats. We want their co-operation and from our experience with other health programs I am convinced we will get it." In this belief he was too sanguine by far.

Douglas understood that the college, as well as many of their member physicians, had misgivings. A negotiator as well as an optimist, he believed that he could make them partners by bringing them into the planning process, persuade them of the benefits of the program for everyone involved, and offer them an arrangement that they would be happy with. Saskatchewan had a history of municipal doctors and local health-insurance schemes that grew out of community initiatives during the Depression. Throughout the 1950s the medical profession in Saskatchewan had built up two non-profit insurance companies, and in some cases whole municipalities purchased coverage. Notwithstanding the challenges that come with any change, Douglas had worked successfully in implementing a huge range of provincial health reforms over the preceding years.

When he made his announcement in 1959, the registrar of the college initially said that despite a few reservations, "I don't think you can quarrel too much with what the premier said." Two days later, however, the college's position had hardened, and it issued a statement saying that "the medical profession of this province has recorded its unanimous opposition to a medical care program ... which is completely under government control." From there forward, the college proceeded to fight the government at every turn.

In early 1960 the college refused to name representatives to the Advisory Planning Committee unless the terms of reference of the committee were changed first. Then in March the college issued a "declaration of rights" of physicians whose terms directly contradicted the government's stated principles guiding universality. Effectively, the college advocated that the government subsidize private insurance where needed, without a full public program (an arrangement similar to that reached in the United States in early 2010). It established an "information committee" whose task was to disseminate publicity opposing the government's plan and levied funds from its members for this purpose.

When finally, after much delay and argument, college representatives were appointed to the committee, they did everything possible to obstruct its progress. Douglas clung, as the McLeods put it, to a "rationalist conviction that with a little more time to get the facts across" he could convince the college that universal medicare was good both for doctors and patients. Douglas underestimated the stubbornness of doctors: they were independent, fiercely protective of their professional autonomy, and just as determined as he was. Also, they were speaking in profoundly different terms. While Douglas's starting point was the public good, the college began its argument from the standpoint of professional autonomy. Suspicion and ill will on the part of the college and frustration on both sides soon made this gap a chasm.

Also weighing against the premier was the effect of some recent changes in the physician mix in the province, which Douglas had perhaps not factored in. Saskatchewan had recently had an influx of British physicians, many of whom had come to Canada specifically to avoid working within their newly implemented National Health Service. The college had recently been taken over by urban specialists, and Saskatchewan's old-fashioned country doctors had lost their influence. The country doctors who knew and better understood the CCF and the province's co-operative tradition might have been more receptive to universal health insurance, but the physicians who now controlled the college were unyielding.

Tensions grew in the 1960 provincial election campaign, in which medicare became a key issue. "When Douglas appeared on a Regina television forum in March 1960," the McLeods write, "a doctor asked him how he could pretend the Advisory Committee was really studying the issue when the government had already made up its mind. Douglas suggested that if the people wanted to avoid medicare, they should vote against the government." Interestingly, the American Medical Association as well as the Canadian Medical Association entered the election fray, producing propaganda that can be most kindly described as scaremongering. They warned that doctors would flee the province, that patients would be "reduced to a number," that doctors would be forced to give patients' confidential information to the government, that the CCF would bring "the garbage of Europe" to work as doctors, and that bureaucrats would commit women with menopausal symptoms to insane asylums. Fifty years later the American debate over

Obama's proposed health-care reforms raged with equal irrationality.

The Saskatchewan College of Physicians and Surgeons raised and spent more than $100,000 on anti-medicare publicity in the campaign, far more than any political party. At least $35,000 came from organizations outside the province, worried that Saskatchewan was setting a dangerous precedent. To put these sums in context, in the 1962 federal election, the newborn child of the CCF and labour organizations, the New Democratic Party, ran a federal election campaign with a budget of $116,000. The anti-medicare propaganda was so ridiculous that it was widely disbelieved by the public, thus strengthening the government's case. The 1960 election sent the CCF back into power with its fifth consecutive majority.

Although the CCF was returned to office with a clear public mandate to proceed on medicare, relations with the doctors went from bad to worse. The health minister, J. Walter Erb, mismanaged the ongoing discussions. Despite the quiet urging of several other members of cabinet, Douglas refused to fire him, displaying his typical loyalty to his subordinates. The college representatives continued to subvert the Advisory Planning Committee on Medical Care, whose report Douglas wished to have in hand before passing a legislative bill. The committee chair, Dr. Walter Thompson, the retired president of the University of Saskatchewan, was so frustrated by the obstructionism that he asked Douglas if he could resign. Douglas persuaded him to stay, writing to him that he was sure "some common understanding" might be reached. Douglas was less diplomatic in private. Those close to him recall that he was furious that the college, the professional body that should have been most concerned with the welfare of patients, was obstructing his heartfelt efforts to do the best for those same people. The college's power over its members was such that those physicians who privately supported medicare could not be persuaded to say so publicly.

In August 1961 Douglas assumed the federal leadership of the New Democratic Party, stepped down from the premier's chair, and Woodrow Lloyd became premier. Although Douglas withdrew from the spotlight at this point, medicare's birth remains very much his story. He was a vocal advocate for the program's implementation throughout the drama that continued to unfold.

Premier Lloyd immediately passed the Medical Care Insurance Act in the legislature, moved Erb to public works, and appointed William Davies to take his place as health minister. Over the winter of 1961 talks with the doctors stalled once more. Davies formed the new Medical Care Insurance Commission (MCIC), approached a number of popular doctors to serve on the board, but was only able to recruit one practising physician. Others told him that the college would "come down on them like a ton of bricks" if they sat on the commission. Two non-practising physicians sat on the committee—the deputy minister of health and an academic.

July 1962 saw the conflict come to a head in a bitter doctors' strike. Physicians moved seriously ill patients out of the province prior to withdrawing their labour and continued to provide emergency service; they did not neglect the care of the acutely ill, but they did not deliver regular care. They demanded that the newly passed Medical Care Insurance Act be revoked or suspended before they would negotiate. The strike was widely covered by Canadian and international media. The wild and unsupportable claims of the anti-medicare camp and the evident reasonableness of the government plan meant that by the end of the month, the majority of media opinion had crystallized in support of the government. The main criticism in the national and international press was that the college refused to negotiate in good faith with the government, and that it demanded that a democratically elected government repeal legislation in order to begin dialogue. The main exceptions to this view were the Saskatchewan daily newspapers, which were supportive of the college and opposed to the government.

The twenty-three days of the physicians' strike were a divisive time in Saskatchewan. Everyone knew of someone who suffered because they were unable to access their regular medical practitioner. Those who generally opposed the CCF seized on the drama to criticize the government on many fronts. As the strike wore on, some physicians who had moral and professional misgivings about withdrawing their services began to quietly open their doors, so that by the end of July roughly half of the province's 900 or so doctors were providing medical care, in addition to 110 freshly recruited physicians from outside the province. The standoff between the college and the MCIC persisted, with both sides exasperated and exhausted.

At this point Lloyd, emulating Douglas, sought the assistance of the best possible outside expert to resolve the crisis. Lord Taylor, a British psychiatrist, was a Labourite who had earned his peerage for his role in developing the National Health Service. He agreed to serve, on the understanding that rather than a monetary payment he would be given a fishing trip in northern Saskatchewan. When he arrived in Regina on July 16, in the dark depths of the strike, Taylor expressed sympathy for both sides, announced that he would not serve as the premier's adviser as expected, and that he intended to mediate between the cabinet and the college despite not having been asked to do so. Taylor spoke with all major players in a series of meetings and discussions, kept the government and the college strictly separate, and soon established his control of the situation. The eccentric and forceful doctor was a theatrical presence as much as a mediator. He insisted on parking in the no-parking zone at his hotel, leaving a piece of House of Lords stationary under the windshield as justification, and got away with it. He listened, cajoled, sympathized, raged, and became so central to the process that he broke impasses with the doctors by threatening to go home. On July 23 Taylor announced at a press conference that an agreement between the college and the government had been signed.

Soon, despite all the hysteria that had preceded the law's passage, Saskatchewan's physicians were quite happy with the system. Despite the dire predictions, no one interfered with doctors' medical decisions, or forced them to reveal patients' secrets. They no longer needed to hire collection agencies to chase their patients, and bills were paid promptly. On average, physicians' incomes actually increased under the CCF's scheme. The public did not soon lose the sour taste that the bitter battle had precipitated, however, and some say that the conflict sowed the seeds of the CCF's defeat to the Liberals in 1964—their first loss in two decades. Even so, the Liberal government that took power made no changes to the insurance plan. One of the doctors who was a key strategist opposing the plan, Efstathios Barootes, later became a Conservative senator and an ardent defender of medicare, saying afterwards, "I have changed my mind."

DOUGLAS'S ACHIEVEMENT in introducing medicare in Saskatchewan represented a deep conceptual shift that radically altered the provision of health care in Canada. He convinced a nation that in a civilized society, health care should be considered essential to individual and social well-being, and viewed both as a public right and a collective obligation.

However, the events surrounding the birth of universal health insurance in Canada were full of irony on several levels, the first being economic. Douglas came to power in an impoverished, bankrupt province. He couldn't immediately deliver the full range of the CCF's program for social democracy within a broken economy. As the province's private and public finances strengthened, his government pressed forward with social innovations and ultimately universal health insurance. Medicare might have been more appealing to doctors when Saskatchewan was poor. After all, municipal plans had flourished during the Depression, when few citizens could afford to pay their doctor's bills, and town doctors then preferred some government financial backing.

From the perspective of labour relations, a great irony was that the CCF—the party synonymous in Canada with workers' rights to organize and strike—found itself importing strikebreakers in the form of replacement doctors from outside the province. Expressed in this measure was the notion that even labour rights, an area of staunch CCF support, had limits within society. In this case the government's obligation to ensure the delivery of essential services could, and did, trump the rights of a group of workers to collectively deprive the public of those essential services.

In yet another twist of fate, though this program would be his proudest achievement, Douglas's political fortunes suffered no greater short-term blow than during the birth of medicare. After almost two decades had been spent building Saskatchewan's economy, civil service, social services, the political legitimacy of the CCF, and his own credibility as premier, the birth of medicare in Saskatchewan should have been a crowning achievement for Douglas. Instead, the surrounding events meant that he left provincial politics in circumstances of conflict and failed to win his federal seat in Regina in 1962. Douglas put all his political capital on the line for what he believed and paid a hefty political price in the short term. He was eventually proved to be right and initiated an essential feature of Canadian society, the universal public insurance of medical services.

The last irony is that though Canadians treasure medicare as it is, it exists as a mere portion of what Douglas and the CCF envisaged. The greatest successes of the idealistic Douglas government were forged from an amalgam of fairness and sound planning. In the difficult circumstances of its birth, medicare achieved an equitable way to pay for services rather than a properly planned system to care for health. It did so with an emphasis on acute medical care over preventive health, though CCF platforms had often prioritized prevention ahead of cure. Perhaps if the birth of the Saskatchewan medicare system had been a functional collaboration between government and physicians, more planning could have been undertaken, resulting in a more complete health-care system as an example for the nation to emulate.

For the rest of his life, Douglas would point out that while medicare had removed the financial barrier from the interaction between doctor and patient, that was only meant to be the first step. To this day, Canadian health care does not include a national, comprehensive planning process to address issues such as goal-setting, appropriate distribution of limited health-care resources, the uniform use of the best scientific knowledge, or preparations for constantly changing health-care needs. As Bob Rae put it, "On health care, he was a real visionary. He believed that where we're at now is just a kind of a half-way house.... He would have pushed much harder to get the system to keep moving in a different direction."

Nevertheless, the CCF's achievement of medicare in Saskatchewan was momentous. Liberal governments in Ottawa would preside over the nationwide implementation of medicare and take full credit for it. The process was not a quick one. Not until 1968, with persistent prodding by Douglas and the NDP, did medicare come into existence across Canada. And it was only in 1984 that the Canada Health Act gave full form to the federal–provincial arrangement. There are some who believe that Canada was on track to have a universal health-care system regardless of the role played by the CCF and later the NDP. Others come to more pointed conclusions. As the journalist and historian Walter Stewart writes, "People may believe that the Liberals would have produced a universal medicare system even without the example the CCF set in Saskatchewan, but then, many people believe that Elvis is still alive."

CHAPTER 9

Return to Ottawa, 1961–71

My grandmother, who was a very fine Scots lady... had such long beautiful hair that her boast was that she could sit on her hair. Now I have a daughter who can't sit on her skirts. There is a generation gap.... Of course young people are changing, but I want to say one thing to you: Don't sell these young people short. Do not be fooled by beards and mini-skirts and long hair. This is a generation of young people who are not just thinking of how they can be a president of General Motors; this is a generation of young people who are concerned about the war in Viet Nam and Cambodia, who are concerned about the Negroes in the United States and the Indians in Canada, who are concerned about the poor and disadvantaged, who are going down into the slums and ghettos to fight the battles of the underprivileged. I think this generation is going to do a great job. I believe that the New Democratic Party and the Canadian Labour Congress will give them the kind of leadership and the kind of help to transform this society into a society which will have a greater appreciation of human values and a greater measure of social justice.

—TOMMY DOUGLAS ADDRESSING THE 1970 CONVENTION OF THE CANADIAN LABOUR CONGRESS

When Douglas returned to federal politics after his long tenure in Saskatchewan, he traded the power of the premiership for an opposition seat. He went from running a province with a majority government, surrounded by a highly motivated, professional staff, to squeaking into Parliament in a by-election to lead a minor party there.

Yet it is clear that over his ensuing seventeen years in Parliament, Tommy Douglas's influence on Canadian life was very real. Without ever holding the reins of power, he and the New Democratic Party had a significant effect on discourse and policy, impressing on the House that humanity must underlie politics, that Canada should make planned strategic decisions in order to be a strong and independent nation, and that a strong nation should apply itself to strive for good.

NATIONALLY, THE CCF'S high wartime approval rating faded after the Allied victory. The party's calls for economic planning seemed less important in the healthy postwar economy. A 1956 statement of principles, the Winnipeg Declaration, superseded the Regina Manifesto in more cautious terms. The bedrock concepts were still that society and the economy must be operated for human benefit first, not primarily for profit. At the same time the new document made it clear that there was a place for private industry within a social democracy, as Douglas had demonstrated in Saskatchewan. George Cadbury wrote Douglas, congratulating him because the national CCF was learning from the "sane wisdom" of his provincial government. However, this moderated stance both failed to catch the imagination of the broad electorate and alienated some hard-liners who believed that the CCF no longer represented their views.

Although Douglas felt as many did that farmers and labourers were natural political allies, the CCF's base remained mainly in rural western Canada. Meanwhile, Canada was changing from a highly agrarian to a predominantly urban society. From 1900 to 1960 the proportion of Canadians who lived and worked on farms fell from 50 to 14 percent of the population. Many believed that if the CCF was to grow into more than a regional party, it needed to represent labour. David Lewis, national president of the CCF since 1954, was a major proponent of this view. He and others set about to reinvent the CCF as a new national entity with an influx of labour support, and thus the New Democratic Party was born.

David Lewis thought Douglas should be the first leader of the NDP. He thought that Douglas's profile and political brilliance gave the new party the best shot at a successful start. Douglas agreed that national renewal was needed but thought that Lewis should be the leader. Lewis had several obvious advantages: he had worked closely with both the national CCF and labour leaders like Claude Jodoin, who had a hand in designing the new party. Lewis told his own family that he didn't think Canada was ready for a Jewish national party leader. Lewis was both bilingual and a lawyer, and Douglas believed a national leader should have such ability and experience. He himself had neither of these. Also, he was hesitant to leave Saskatchewan and protested that there was still much work to do there, and he wanted to finish it. Coldwell, the long-standing federal CCF leader, was bowing out of active political life for health reasons.

When he finally agreed to put his name forward, Douglas won the leadership of the new NDP on a hot summer day in 1961 at an enthusiastic convention in Ottawa. He accepted the position with mixed feelings. He knew that a return to federal politics would be a tough slog. He was motivated more by duty than a sense of personal ambition, viewing himself as part of a movement that was larger than himself or anyone in it. Of his decision to return to Ottawa, he wrote to a friend, "We must either break through or lose the beachhead ... the time has come to go for broke."

Despite the jubilant mood of the founding convention,

the NDP had neither the money nor the organization needed to field an effective campaign in the upcoming federal election. And in addition to trying to build up the NDP nationally, Douglas carried his responsibilities as premier through the remainder of 1961. This was a tense and difficult period, as he tried to prepare for the federal scene and manage the medicare battle.

Over the winter of 1961–62 he kept up a brutal pace, travelling and speaking all over the country for the NDP. The nascent party needed him everywhere, and he tried to be everywhere. Tommy Shoyama went with him, his sole staff, serving as travel coordinator, baggage handler, policy adviser, and purveyor of chicken soup when Douglas fell ill. Shoyama recalled, "We'd go any place there was some possibility or expression of interest—like Truro, Nova Scotia. How come? Because who was there but a United Church minister, who had come of course from Saskatchewan. Same thing in Hawkesbury, Ontario."

That winter Douglas campaigned on a platform that in retrospect looked like the next chapter in Canadian history. The NDP's proposals included a national Bill of Rights, an augmented system of old-age pensions, a bilingual civil service, a new federal–provincial tax arrangement, an increase in international aid, the recognition of Communist China, and universal health care for all Canadians. While the party's ideas were prescient, its campaign was underfunded. Its leader's oratorical skill could not overcome either the new party's structural weaknesses or its empty coffers. Labour, the much-chased bride to the CCF's ardent suitor, had a large delegate presence at the NDP founding convention, then became coy during the election campaign, as if waiting to see how things would turn out. The groundswell union of labour and farmers was nowhere to be seen.

In Saskatchewan the NDP campaign of 1962 was reminiscent of the tooth-and-nail fighting of Douglas's early political career but without the grassroots support. In Regina his campaign rallies were met by counter-rallies staged by Keep Our Doctors, a vocal group of medicare opponents. To greet the Douglas campaign motorcades, some homeowners displayed coffins on their front lawns. The campaign car was sometimes assaulted by people hurling stones, swinging fists, cursing and spitting. Ed Whelan, Douglas's campaign manager, received nightly telephone death threats by someone who shouted, "I'll shoot you, you Red Bastard!" This was unheard of in Saskatchewan, a province that prided itself on its neighbourliness. Meanwhile, the old CCF faithful were unsure about their new marriage to labour, worried that the party was being taken over by eastern unions.

The election on June 18, 1962, fell just before the impending doctors' strike in Saskatchewan. Douglas's cross-country campaigning had left the CCF stronghold in Saskatchewan vulnerable. Both the NDP and Douglas were punished in that federal election for the provincial CCF's unyielding determination to introduce universal health insurance. Across Canada, rather than the forty- or fifty-member caucus he had hoped for, Douglas saw only nineteen NDP members elected, and he was not one of them. He appeared briefly on television and quoted a ballad, "I'll lay me down and bleed awhile, and then I'll rise and fight again."

DOUGLAS WAS SOMETIMES WISTFUL about his decision to leave Saskatchewan. Toward the end of his life he said, "I think a lot of people, and they may have been right, a lot of people thought I should have stayed. I had a nice, comfortable set up, I was a Premier, had a very popular cabinet ... and why in heaven's name should we be worrying about the socialist movement in Canada as a whole? What we were going to do, trying to make the party come alive, just didn't interest them. Maybe they were right too. Maybe we were trying to push the thing too fast."

Shortly after Douglas lost the Regina seat, he received a phone call from Erhart Regier, the NDP member who had just been elected for the fourth time to represent Burnaby-Coquitlam in British Columbia. Regier, who was originally from Saskatchewan, was very upset by Douglas's defeat in Regina and offered to resign so that Douglas could contest his seat in a by-election. Douglas refused, telling Regier to sober up. Soon Douglas read in the newspaper that Regier had asked the Speaker of the House to declare his seat vacant. In accordance with Regier's request, the NDP executive of Burnaby-Coquitlam invited Douglas to contest the by-election, which he won.

He knew that there was little chance of the NDP forming the federal government in his lifetime. Nonetheless, he believed that if democratic socialism was to realize its broad goals in Canada, it had to be a national movement. As premier, Douglas had undertaken huge innovations within the provincial sphere. However, there was a limit to what could be done at the provincial level without the purviews of monetary, trade, or foreign policy. At the federal level he could speak to these issues directly, but without his party in power, his arguments had limited force.

About this time the federal Liberals began what would become a long-standing practice of appropriating much of the socialists' platform for themselves. Events of recent years had caused them to reconsider their place in Canadian politics. The 1957 federal election, in which Diefenbaker and the Progressive Conservative Party overturned twenty-two years of Liberal rule to win a minority government, had been one of the great upsets in Canadian political history. Liberal hubris, and the party's sense of its entitlement to rule, were so entrenched that the Liberal leader, Lester Pearson, gave a speech in the House of Commons in which he stated that the Conservatives were unfit to govern and asked Diefenbaker to voluntarily restore power to the Liberals. In response, Diefenbaker called a snap election and transformed his minority into the largest majority government to that time in Canadian history, with 208 seats in the House of Commons. The Liberals emerged with 49, their worst count ever.

Smarting from this humiliation, Pearson set about re-evaluating the future of the Liberal Party. The Liberals understood the threat posed by the CCF as keenly as they felt their defeat by the Conservatives. In September 1960 the Liberals held a policy convention in Kingston, at which the attendees included socialists and labour representatives. J. Wendell Macleod, dean of medicine at the University of Saskatchewan, and popularly known as "Saskatchewan's Red Dean," delivered a paper on hospital and medical care. Much effort was expended to secure the participation of Claude Jodoin, the union leader who within a year would hoist Tommy Douglas into the air alongside David Lewis at the NDP's founding convention. Other key labour figures were also included, and many observers felt that the Liberals were seeking to weaken the growing affinity between organized labour and the CCF.

At the Kingston conference, the Liberal strategist Tom Kent advocated a comprehensive, wide-ranging social security system including government-financed medicare. A subsequent Liberal rally in early 1961 confirmed what the press had already anticipated, namely, the party's new "tangible move to the left to stave off attack from the New Party (NDP)." The Liberal's "Plan for Health," the most hotly debated item on the agenda, promised universal access to health care irrespective of ability to pay, and was criticized by some within the Liberal Party as being too similar to the socialized medicine of the Saskatchewan CCF.

In this manner the NDP pushed national discourse toward innovations like those the CCF had successfully pioneered in Saskatchewan. On his return to Ottawa, Douglas became both the conscience and guardian of medicare nationally. In 1960 Diefenbaker had created a commission headed by Justice Emmett Hall to examine the idea of medicare. The Hall Commission reported in 1964, with a glowing assessment of the success of the CCF initiative in

Saskatchewan and advocating its adoption throughout Canada. Douglas called the report "the finest statement on medicare that has ever been published in the English language." The Liberals, now back in power, appeared for some time to be in danger of retreating to their time-worn practice of promising medicare in elections without delivering once in office. Because of Pearson's lack of action, Douglas introduced a non-confidence motion in 1964, and then again in 1965. The Liberals survived both votes with the support of the Social Credit Party, and finally in 1966 the Liberals introduced a bill to share health-care costs with the provinces, which was approved 177 to 2 in the House of Commons. They promised to start by July 1, 1967, but then delayed implementation for another year. They had to figure out how to bring on board the provinces, some of which were opposed to the program. The funding solution was ultimately devised by Al Johnson. A seasoned Saskatchewan bureaucrat and early Tommy Douglas hire, he had been deputy provincial secretary in Saskatchewan when medicare was introduced there, was now assistant deputy minister of finance in Ottawa, and was a notable member of the Saskatchewan Mafia. The legislation came into effect on July 1, 1968.

DOUGLAS WOULD BE a federal member of Parliament for another seventeen years, as long as he had been premier. Though deeply respected both for his integrity and intellect by compatriots and opponents alike, he may have given too much credit to the people of Canada in thinking they would pay attention to politicians' actual statements and positions.

He grew into politics in the 1930s, when people travelled across the countryside for hours to attend political rallies that routinely went past midnight. As a CCF politician in the Prairies Douglas was loved by people who either believed fervently in the cause of democratic socialism or were ready to challenge it and debate for hours. They really did review the steps taken by their politicians. Douglas had a wonderfully warm, reassuring radio presence that reached out through a cold prairie night as he signed off his addresses with an expression from wartime London, "Good night, and good luck."

As an opposition voice Douglas was both an intellectual force and a confident wit, and held the resonant power of his moral and intellectual convictions. However, by the time he returned to Ottawa, the era of television, of image-making and "spin," had arrived. He was less magnetic on television than the charismatic Diefenbaker, less alluring than the dashing Trudeau. Arena rallies and full-fledged speeches, his strengths, were less crucial as the morning press conference and the "sound bite" became the main vehicles of political communication. Douglas wanted to turn the party over to a younger generation, while the party faithful still clamoured to keep him.

In the youth movement of these years, Douglas saw kindred spirits. He felt that the radicals of the 1960s and '70s were kin to himself and his friends Mark Talnicoff and Stanley Knowles as young men. Douglas understood the motivations of the peace protesters. He had once been a young rebel running off to theological school, dreaming of a world in which moral principles and human values would replace the capitalist imperative of profit irrespective of human cost. As social gospellers they had asked the same questions as this new generation of seekers. *Why do the wealthy take from the poor? Can we structure the economy more humanely? What kind of system will allow people to co-operate for the common good?*

Douglas became a sort of grandfatherly patron of the 1960s counterculture. Photos of him from that era often show the trim, grey-haired politician with a peace button on the lapel of his suit. Tie-dyed clothing, men with long hair, and girls with short skirts did not trouble him. He was not one to scold on such matters, not when the superpowers had within his lifetime amassed enough nuclear weapons to wipe out every living thing on the planet. Douglas was categorically anti-nuke at a time when the other Canadian parties were embarrassingly confused on the issue, unable to sort out whether to allow the United States to station nuclear missiles in Canada. Douglas condemned the American war in Vietnam, routinely spoke at anti-war rallies, and did not spare the Canadian munitions industry that sold the U.S. Army $300 million in armaments annually during that conflict. He met with representatives from the Vietnamese National Liberation Front and joined a committee along with the author Farley Mowat and René Lévesque to send medical supplies to North Vietnam while American bombers pulverized it in a horrific bombing campaign.

Douglas's big-picture position on world insecurity was, "I think that the most powerful weapon of all for establishing the rule of law and peace in the world is for the 'have' nations of the world to increase tremendously their contributions, their economic and financial contribution to the people who live in the 'have-not' nations of the world." He supported the liberation of colonies from their European masters, the civil rights movement in America, and the freedom of expression of dissidents. He looked into the future and warned of the growing power of multinational corporations to control pricing and influence purchasing behaviour. Although steadfastly committed to the principles of social democracy, Douglas was quite ready to apply them to new issues and challenges that arose with changing times. As Blakeney put it, "He didn't claim to have all the program all laid out in tablets of stone from the mountain. The nature of social democracy was not a fixed body of doctrine, but an approach to problems."

The young generation's frustration with the status quo was familiar to Douglas because he felt it keenly himself. He said, "Sure they're in rebellion against a lot of standards and values and well they might be. They have got sick and tired of a manipulated society. They may go to extremes at times but this is a generation with more social concern, with a better understanding of the need for love and involvement and cooperation than certainly any generation I have seen in my lifetime." The NDP, he believed, was naturally the party of this generation of youth, and he saw one of his duties as passing the baton of social democracy on to them. In 1971 he wrote, "The absence of a democratic socialist party in the United States is one of the reasons why the young people there have taken to the streets."

On December 2, 1969, the clash between the counterculture and the establishment struck the Douglas family personally. The Beverly Hills home of Tommy's daughter Shirley and her husband, the actor Donald Sutherland, was raided by Los Angeles police. Shirley was alone with their three children. The police searched the home while Shirley and her eldest son, Tom, were made to stand against a wall. Her two younger children, Kiefer and Rachel, cried alone in a bedroom as the police rifled through their possessions. The police found nothing, but they charged Shirley with conspiracy to obtain a destructive device. Her crime, it seemed, was that she had participated in a fundraising event for Friends of the Black Panthers, which supported a free breakfast program for poor children. The Black Panthers was a radical Black Power movement. Shirley's interest was the breakfast program.

Douglas called a press conference in which he declared that he was certain of Shirley's innocence and said, "I am proud of the fact that my daughter believes, as I do, that hungry children should be fed whether they are Black Panthers or White Republicans." The next day he flew to Los Angeles to be with Shirley. Several months later the charges were thrown out of court. Newspapers put forward a good case that the Los Angeles police had tried to frame Shirley in an effort to scare off middle-class people who might be tempted to lend support to radical causes. Douglas believed that Shirley had also been targeted because her father was a well-known anti-war socialist politician, and he suspected that Canadian and U.S. intelligence agencies had collaborated on the matter.

In 1976 Lyn Goldman, a friend of Shirley's from Regina, by coincidence met a former American intelligence agent at a dinner party in Rio de Janeiro. He indicated that he had worked on Shirley's case, that he had been assigned to monitor Douglas's arrival at the airport in Los Angeles, and that Shirley had been framed not only for her involvement with the Black Panthers but because of her father's political views. He said that it was obvious to everyone involved that Shirley had committed no crime, and his disillusionment arising from this episode led to his eventual departure from intelligence work.

Although she was never convicted of anything, U.S. immigration officials mounted a long, and ultimately successful, campaign to bar Shirley from working in the United States. She was a professional actress, and of course much of the work available to an actress was in the United States. Years later, when asked if he had ever doubted Shirley's innocence, Douglas replied that it had never even occurred to him. After all, his daughter was a lifelong pacifist, whereas he was "basically a fiery Scot."

CHAPTER 10

The October Crisis, 1970

Right now there is no constitution in this country, no Bill of Rights, no provincial constitutions. This government now has the power by Order in Council to do anything it wants—to intern any citizen, to deport any citizen, to arrest any person or to declare any organization subversive or illegal.... I predict that within six months, when the Canadian people have had time to reflect on what has happened today—the removal of all the protection and liberties presently on the statute books of Canada, a country placed under the War Measures Act, regulations introduced allowing persons to be detained for 90 days without a chance to prove their innocence—when that day comes, the Canadian people will look on this as a black Friday for civil liberties in Canada.

—TOMMY DOUGLAS SPEAKING IN PARLIAMENT
ON OCTOBER 16, 1970

When he was young, Douglas saw that a boy could run around in wide-open spaces in Canada much more freely than in his country of birth, and he liked that. From the time he witnessed the breaking of the Winnipeg General Strike, and Estevan's wounded coal-miners, Douglas was on the side of freedom and civil liberties. He had watched the

Nazis marching at Nuremburg in 1936, and after the Second World War he lamented that western capitalist countries achieved a political democracy with no economic democracy, and that communist countries achieved the inverse—economic democracy in totalitarian states. He thought that things should be different, that there could be a social democracy in which government would both participate directly in the economy and regulate a free market. Such a system should be democratic, with human rights and civil liberties at its core.

One of the benefits of being back in opposition in Ottawa instead of running the province of Saskatchewan (a role that required a degree of formality and discretion) was that Douglas felt entirely free to speak his mind. On the subject of Prime Minister Trudeau's marriage to Margaret Sinclair, his comment was, "It is good that Mr. Trudeau did not consult the cabinet. It would probably have insisted on a study session followed by a white paper about which nothing would be done."

In 1968 Canada fell in love with Pierre Trudeau, who then became prime minister. He was our good-looking, smart, and wealthy new prince. The dragon that sometimes puffed smoke in the face of both this prince and English Canada was Quebec's separatist movement. During the 1960s the Front de libération du Québec (FLQ) had conducted a protracted bombing campaign against the Montreal establishment, which had killed six people. The possibility of Quebec's departure from Canada was very much in the air. René Lévesque's separatist Parti Québécois was gaining momentum and credibility. On October 5, 1970, the dragon breathed fire. James Cross, a British diplomat, was kidnapped by a small group of people who claimed to represent the FLQ. The kidnappers' demands included the broadcast of the FLQ manifesto, a ransom payment, the release of francophone "political prisoners," and a plane to fly the kidnappers to either Cuba or Algeria. The government refused. Six days later, the Quebec labour minister, Pierre Laporte—an old school chum of Prime Minister Trudeau's—was kidnapped by another group of people who also claimed to represent the FLQ. On October 15 Trudeau held a late-night meeting with the leaders of the opposition parties—Tommy Douglas, Robert Stanfield of the Progressive Conservatives, and Réal Caouette of the Créditistes (Social Credit in Quebec)—and told them that he would be imposing the War Measures Act early the next morning and would ask Parliament to ratify the decision later in the day.

At four in the morning on October 16, the War Measures Act came into effect. Before dawn, police in Quebec began to raid homes and arrest those suspected of sympathizing with the FLQ. Hundreds of people were arrested without charge. The laws of their country had been changed overnight: they could be held without charge for ninety days. Organizations could be declared subversive or illegal. The Bill of Rights no longer applied. The army mobilized, and Canada was suddenly a police state.

The NDP caucus met later the same morning. Douglas was sombre and brief in addressing the members of his own party regarding the use of the War Measures Act. He said, "My position is to oppose it. I know that some of you may not support me, and I'll understand that. There's no question about it: if the Prime Minister calls an election over this, it may devastate the party. You have your own political careers to think about. I'm going back upstairs now. I have to speak at 11 o'clock. I'm against it, period." Fifteen NDP members stood with their leader, and four decided to support the War Measures Act.

That morning Prime Minister Trudeau stood in Parliament to read grave letters from Mayor Jean Drapeau of Montreal and Premier Robert Bourassa of Quebec supporting Trudeau's actions. Stanfield, leader of the official opposition, rose and gave guarded support of the War Measures Act. Douglas stood to speak. He condemned the kidnappers' actions and supported the government's refusal to succumb to their demands. He acknowledged that the government faced a difficult situation and indicated that he and his party endorsed the government using the armed forces if necessary. However, said Douglas, he and the NDP could not support the imposition of the War Measures Act. To a rising chorus of heckling and catcalls, the NDP leader methodically laid out his case, saying, "We are not prepared to use the preservation of law and order as a smokescreen to destroy the liberties and the freedom of the people of Canada." He pointed out that there were sections in the Criminal Code that gave the government broad powers to deal with treason, sedition, conspiracy, and offensive weapons. He suggested that if these powers were deemed insufficient by the government, its proper course of action would have been to consult Parliament in order to be invested with greater powers. The present course of action, Douglas argued, was an overreaction that legitimized the FLQ and risked fanning the flames of revolutionary violence rather than suppressing it. His position was that of reason and principle: "If we are going to tell people that we value democracy and that democracy is the way of dealing with social change, we must use the democratic procedures and not revert on our part to the very kind of violence which we are condemning on the other side."

For his stance Douglas endured the derision of many Canadians and of his fellow Parliamentarians. One suggested that he had something to be afraid of under the War Measures Act. Others cried, "Shame," and had to be told by the Speaker to sit down so that Douglas could speak. The day after the imposition of the War Measures Act, the body of Pierre Laporte was found in the trunk of a car. Douglas condemned the murder and the murderers but stood steadfastly with his conviction that the civil liberties of Canadians should not also fall victim to these events. The days that followed were heated. Some provincial NDP politicians wrote in support of Douglas, but others sided with the government. Letters and telegrams filled his desk. One correspondent wrote, "It would be a most opportune time to take identical measures against you and your party." A poll by the Canadian Institute of Public Opinion asked Canadians if their assessment of certain politicians had changed. Sixty percent thought more highly of Trudeau, and 5 percent stated that their opinion of him had suffered; 36 percent had a more negative opinion of Douglas, and 8 percent thought more of him. Support for the NDP collapsed to 13 percent nationally in December of that year.

Douglas was unyielding. On an acrimonious television panel he told the Canadian people, "I want to remind you of something. I want to remind you that in the 1940s the government of Canada passed regulations under the War Measures Act to intern all Canadian-born Japanese. I remember being booed off the platform in Vancouver for opposing that. People said, 'The government tells us there's a yellow peril, that these Japs are going to blow up railways and everything.' What happened? We locked them up and confiscated their property. And at the end of the war Mr. King said, 'There is not a single proven case of sabotage by any Canadian-born Japanese.'"

Trudeau evidently understood Douglas's concerns. The day after the declaration of the Act, and Douglas's speech in Parliament, Trudeau wrote a letter to him promising to draft new legislation with a tighter focus, admitting, "Our legal fabric is defective in not enabling the government to deal with the crisis speedily and effectively without invoking powers that may be too broad." Even so, both anglophone and francophone Canada largely accepted the government's assertion that with the two kidnappings, the country was in a state of "apprehended insurrection," and this justified the suspension of civil liberties. In Quebec 81 percent of people favoured the War Measures Act. Membership in Lévesque's Parti Québécois was almost cut in half. Caouette called for the kidnappers to be executed by firing squad.

In considering Douglas's stance during the October Crisis, it is worth noting that Quebec's issues were foreign to him, unlike, for instance, the problems of struggling prairie farmers. He sympathized with the grievances of working Quebecers, but felt that their fundamental problems were ones of justice and economic oppression, not simply language. Lévesque and the Parti Québécois were social democrats, but they wished to break from Canada, and Douglas believed in a strong central government. Despite valiant efforts, Douglas's spoken French was atrocious. He was in every way an outsider to French-speaking Canada. Therefore, his stance during the October Crisis was motivated not by politics or affinity with a particular group but by a deep respect for civil rights. Addressing the Manitoba NDP convention during the crisis, he quoted Pastor Martin Niemöller: "When the Nazis came to get the Communists, I remained silent. When they came to get the socialists, I remained silent.... When they came to get the Jews, I remained silent. When they came to get me, there was no one left to speak."

Despite Trudeau's conciliatory letter, the government made no concessions in response to the NDP's request for some protection of civil liberties. Of the 450 Canadians hastily arrested under the War Measures Act, only one was convicted of a crime. A murder had been committed, but no evidence of the government's claimed "apprehended insurrection" was ever produced. Although analysts of the 1970 October Crisis would later widely agree that Trudeau had overreacted, as it unfolded, Douglas and the NDP stood almost alone in opposition to the War Measures Act. In 1970 Douglas staked his ground where he thought it was right. He could not see any justification for the suspension of civil liberties, so he stood with those whose rights he believed were being violated, willing to endure popular hatred, unbending at his party's heavy political costs, to stand steadfast for the sake of moral convictions.

CHAPTER 11

Looking to the Future, 1971–86

> I now urge you to go out and work as you have never
> worked before because this country is at the crossroads
> between social justice or social disaster, and the little bit
> we do here could be the turning point ... we can play our
> part in bringing about the day that every democratic
> socialist dreams of: the day when all men, every race,
> colour, and creed, will sit each below their own fig tree
> and none shall make them afraid.
> —TOMMY DOUGLAS, SPEAKING AT THE NOMINATING
> CONVENTION IN PARKSVILLE, BRITISH COLUMBIA, TO ELECT
> HIS SUCCESSOR ON OCTOBER 2, 1977

Douglas maintained the idealism of his youth even as he
entered the last decades of his life. His mannerisms were
sometimes quaint, those of a previous generation. One
might say that in his golden years, he carried himself like an
old-fashioned young man. His energy and work ethic were
legendary. Cliff Scotton, NDP national secretary, complained that he could not match Douglas's stamina. "I would
come back from a trip with him worn out, dragged down

and he'd be still dancing about. He's as resilient as a wire spring." Hans Brown, who started work as Douglas's executive assistant in 1969, when Douglas was sixty-five years old, said, "He worked at a ferocious pace and he liked to be sure that everybody else was working ferociously too.... I never saw anything like him. It made me tired just watching him running upstairs." His political ethic had not changed either. Brown said, "He's interested in getting things done. Translating philosophy into action. Practical programs for people and the whole process of persuading people to raise their sights, to go after things that may be a little tough but can be got if you really put your mind to it."

In his last speech as leader of the New Democratic Party, Douglas quoted from one of J.S. Woodsworth's prayers: "May we be the children of the brighter and better day which even now is beginning to dawn. May we not impede, but rather co-operate with the great spiritual forces which we believe are impelling the world onward and upward. For our supreme task is to make our dreams come true and to transform our city into the Holy City—to make this land in reality 'God's own country.'" If Douglas sounded sometimes like a preacher in his political speeches, he did so comfortably, for he had faith in the importance of his work on earth.

When he gave up the leadership of the NDP to David Lewis in 1971, he became energy critic, remaining in that position through most of the 1970s, a tumultuous decade for energy policy and pricing. Douglas argued that oil was a resource of key national strategic importance and advocated a Canadian-centred energy policy in this vital arena. He called for greater public ownership and control over Canadian energy resources and production, for more public investment to be deployed to retain research and processing jobs in Canada, and asserted that the public, rather than the large multinational companies, should derive a greater share of energy profits as world oil prices climbed. He believed that the nation's need for energy security was a compelling argument for public involvement. These positions seem as relevant today as they were then.

During the energy crisis of 1973, the NDP held the balance of power with a Trudeau minority government. Douglas urged federal action to preserve domestic oil supply for Canadian rather than U.S. needs, and to create a publicly owned petroleum company to defend Canadian oil interests. Frustrated by months of inaction on the issue, Douglas and Lewis eventually agreed that the NDP would have to bring down the government unless it took action on energy. Trudeau was informed. The following day Trudeau announced initiatives that would meet all the NDP's demands. When Trudeau had finished speaking, Douglas turned to his fellow MP Bill Knight and said, "Well, how do you like that? He hardly missed a word." Out of this, Petro-Canada was born. As was often the case, Douglas was able to shift the energy discourse. Many of his ideas were implemented, but often in half-measure.

It was Douglas who pushed for and eventually succeeded in spurring the creation of the Canada Development Corporation, though it was a such a pale shadow of what he imagined it should be that he was very critical of its incarnation under Trudeau. Douglas was a firm believer in Canadian independence from the United States. Canadians had to control their own policies regarding resources, finance, foreign affairs, and trade if the nation was to define its own identity. Critics grumbled that he was anti-American. The truth was that he spoke on many occasions against driving out U.S. investors and opposed trade prejudices in the form of "artificial barriers against foreign capital, or in discrimination against foreign firms." Rather, he felt it was Canadians' responsibility to assert more influence over their economy with new investment and initiatives. He spent far less time criticizing the United States than he did questioning Canadian politicians about having given in with little negotiation to the interests of large corporations, many of which happened to be American. "I like the Americans," said Douglas. "I have relatives who are Americans, but I don't want them moving into my house and taking over every room until I have to sleep in the basement." Ahead of his time, he also called frequently for environmental protections long before environmentalism became fashionable.

Although he attacked political opponents with scathing wit, Douglas was always generous and kind at an individual level. He had a warm rapport with fellow legislators from all parties, because he was always interested in connecting with people and getting to know them. When Ken More, the Tory who had delivered Douglas's crushing 1962 electoral defeat in Regina, became ill during a parliamentary trip and was admitted to hospital in Moscow, it was Douglas who stayed with him while the rest of their colleagues carried on. He went out of his way to credit Diefenbaker with implementing national hospital insurance and Pearson with putting national medicare into operation. These observations were true, and gentlemanly. The generosity was not returned. The Liberal Party invariably claimed national medicare as its achievement without mentioning the man and the party who first fought the battle to prove that it could be done.

Douglas would spend hours speaking with young NDP candidates and giving them advice. He took a personal interest in the careers of a new generation of young politicians, like Ed Broadbent and Bob Rae. As a high school student in the late 1950s, Broadbent heard Douglas speak in Oshawa and later recalled, "I was totally inspired by the man. I heard his wit, I witnessed his passion, I saw him present a rational argument as he always did, unlike right wing populism or left wing populism." When Broadbent (NDP MP from 1968 to 1990 and 2004 to 2006, NDP national leader from 1975 to 1989) later worked alongside Douglas, he found his youthful admiration to be justified. "He was a man of intelligence, compassion, and gloriously self-mocking wit…. Douglas made politics joyful."

When Bob Rae (an NDP MP from 1978 to 1982, when he became Ontario NDP leader, then the premier of Ontario from 1990 to 1995, and a Liberal MP from 2008 to the present) ran in Toronto in 1978 and asked Douglas if he could appear at one of his campaign events, Douglas replied, "I'll walk down the Danforth naked if it'll help you get elected." This did not prove to be necessary. Rae sat in federal caucus with Douglas, under Broadbent's leadership, and recalls, "His main thing to me was to say, 'We have to be practical. This is what we're trying to get here. This is how

far we want to get. This is what we're bargaining with....
One of his bugaboos was people in caucus who were putting
forward proposals that he thought were unrealistic." Thus, a
veteran politician coached a new generation in his art. As
Rae recalled, "He was not a wild-eyed dreamer. In caucus
meetings he was very tough-minded, very prudent, and very
risk-averse, but it was his toughness that was the thing I had
the deepest impression of."

In the 1970s, after he was released from his duties as
party leader, Douglas became more social again. He and
Irma held spirited dinner parties at their home in Ottawa.
His personal assistant, Richard McLellan, lived across the
street with his then-partner, Jean-Yves Paquet. They were
frequent guests, along with Ottawa politicians and notables.
The Douglases were a formidable pair and generous hosts—
they would each get through perhaps one or two glasses of
wine over a whole evening, while constantly refilling their
guests' glasses.

WE THINK OF DOUGLAS principally as the founder of medicare,
but he helped define this nation in ways that are less recognized. An innovator in civil service, he showed in
Saskatchewan what effect good public management could
have on citizens' quality of life. Blakeney said of him, "I tend

to believe that Douglas had a few areas of uncommon genius. One was that he understood that a good administration was necessary to make a government work. He got for himself very fine administration and in so doing he changed the nature of the public service … by 1950, many would say Saskatchewan had the best provincial public service in Canada."

It was Douglas and Romeo Mathieu of the Quebec CCF executive who first proposed the creation of a National Commission on Bilingualism and Biculturalism. Their list of suggested commissioners included then-CCF supporter and labour activist Pierre Trudeau. (Trudeau's switch from CCF lawyer and labour activist to Liberal politician always made Douglas a little wary of him.) Pearson later took up the idea of this defining, landmark commission when he became prime minister.

In 1964 a bitter debate on a new national flag dragged on for five weeks, until Douglas chastised the House for wasting time when they should be acting on more pressing issues. He answered the suggestion that the St. George's Cross should be retained on the flag in honour of Canada's Christian heritage by declaring, "St. George's Cross was first used in the Crusade when the kings, barons and knights of Christendom perpetrated murder, raping, and plunder in the name of Christianity.... Let us remember first of all that Christianity is not the only faith in Canada. There are people of Jewish faith, the Mohammedan faith and the Buddhist faith." Douglas was a Baptist minister, but his Canada was inclusive. In his brief speech during the flag debate he spoke in support of Pearson's design of three maple leaves but also suggested that a single maple leaf would better symbolize a unified country. He moved that instead of the flag debate tying up Parliament, a committee should study the question and report back. That committee produced the red-and-white flag with a single maple leaf that we know today. Douglas would have never called himself "the father of our flag" and doubtless thought the issue a minor one, but it seems quietly fitting that he had a hand in the creation of our national emblem.

He might not have grasped for small glories, but NDP policies clearly migrated into Liberal platforms in many areas. The political lineage of initiatives such as nationally owned central banking, a bill of rights, a progressive income tax system that favoured lower-income earners, unemployment insurance, a contributory pension plan, old-age pensions, and universal health insurance can all be traced directly back to the social gospellers, the CCF, and the NDP. A surprising number of these innovations bear the handprint of a certain Baptist minister, either through his pioneering initiatives in Saskatchewan or in his role as first leader of the NDP. Without question, Canada went left in the 1960s and '70s, and it did so under a Liberal banner. The "default position" of Canadian social and economic policy moved from what had been very much a pure capitalist economic system to a socialist national framework that encompassed notions of collective responsibility for public well-being.

Would the Liberals have shifted so decidedly in that direction without the dual stimuli of a pair of Conservative electoral wins and the persistent prodding of the socialists? Our close neighbour, the United States, emerged quite differently from the soul-searching of the 1960s. Without Tommy Douglas and the NDP, would Canada today more closely resemble the United States? There can be no definitive answer. It is fair to say, however, that the direction we took in Canada required some concerted thinking, convincing, and dreaming. One of those dreamers was a very slightly built, big-voiced immigrant preacher who spoke as magnetically on the political stump as he once did from the pulpit, and who could hit as hard in a debate as he once did in a boxing ring.

In 1976 Douglas announced that he would not contest the next federal election. In 1977 he addressed a Parksville,

B.C., convention, where a thousand people came both to hear him speak and to cast their ballots for a candidate to replace him. There, in vintage Douglas fashion, he spent little time speaking of the past and instead exhorted the youth of the party to do their utmost for the cause of social democracy. He opened his speech by saying, "You understand that my role here is simply to kill time until the results come in. And I have no illusions that you are sitting here eagerly waiting to listen to me. You are waiting to hear the results. And so am I.... The fact is that I have felt for some time, and I have said so on hundreds of platforms, that we've got to get young men and women into Parliament. And you can't get young men and women into Parliament if all the old fogies hold on to their constituencies, and particularly the good constituencies. Now, of course, what you can do is you can hang on until some day I drop dead somewhere, and then you can hustle around and find a candidate in a hurry and get through a by-election. I think it is much better this way … I'm not going to be in the House of Commons, but if the oil companies think they're going to get a holiday from Tommy Douglas they're going to be mistaken. And if the rip-off artists in this country think I'm taking a vow of silence they've got another thing coming …"

The socialist movement in Canada emerged out of the

Depression like a field of wildflowers after a prairie fire. Douglas was an especially bright bloom. His movement, first as the CCF, sprang from an economically devastated region of Canada and became a nationwide socialist party within a generation—the Canadian New Democratic Party. It did so almost entirely on the sheer strength of humanist ideals and tangible goals that mattered to everyday people. In doing so, the political discourse of our country was transformed.

Douglas was an idealist who did not fall into the trap of being an ideologue. He was a dreamer who imagined practical solutions and lit the flame of dreams in others. As a leader he could synthesize the ideas of those around him but was not shy about demanding the best from them. He was always oriented toward furthering the movement, advancing the goal that society should be structured so that people could make life better for one another. His particular weapon in this quest was what Graeme Gibson, an NDP campaigner in the 1960s, described as "the unique mixture of his ruthless intellect, and folksy humour." Toward the end of his life, amused that he had become respectable, Douglas said, "I don't mind being a symbol but I don't want to be a monument. There are monuments all over the Parliament Buildings and I've seen what the pigeons do to them."

At the Dominion-Provincial Conference in 1946, early in

his tenure as premier of Saskatchewan, he said, "A country's greatness can be measured by what it does for its unfortunates. By that criterion Canada certainly does not stand in the forefront of the nations of the world, although there are signs that we are becoming conscious of our deficiencies and are determined to atone for lost time." Douglas devoted his forty-five years in Canadian politics to addressing these deficiencies and must be judged by that criterion to be a great Canadian.

A social gospeller from start to finish, Douglas was pleased that social activism enjoyed a resurgence in the mainstream of Christian churches late in his life. At that time, he reflected, "The universe isn't made up of a great cruel God who tells everyone what to do, or of a great organization called the Church that steps with relentless heel on anyone who doesn't do what it tells them to do.... Jesus was in his day, and he hasn't been surpassed since, a great moral teacher who recognized man's place in society, the kind of society that man could build ... that the great motivating force in society is love for your fellow man ... and that there is something that for want of a better term they call the Kingdom of God, which is simply an association of people who have certain ideas in common."

In retirement Tommy and Irma remained in Ottawa and

spent more time at their cottage in Wakefield, Quebec, a short drive from the capital. Douglas's idea of slowing down at the cottage was to busy himself by chopping firewood, stacking it, planting young trees on his land, and swimming in the river. All his life he had worn and treasured a gold ring that his father had once given him. One afternoon, suddenly forlorn, he told Irma that he had lost his ring while swimming. The next morning, when the water was still, Irma went out with a stick and found it for him.

Supporters proposed to buy him and Irma a new house or a car as the party's gesture of appreciation, and they declined the offers. Instead, Douglas directed them to use the money to start a foundation to advance social democracy; the Douglas-Coldwell Foundation is still in active operation today.

He had more time to be a grandfather. His grandchildren visited at the cottage, where he taught them to swim, split wood, and drive a car. They knew of their grandfather's political life, but when they visited Tommy and Irma, Granddad focused his full attention on them and had an intent, genuine way of engaging them. "He would make me feel like he had all the time in the world for me," said the actor Kiefer Sutherland. "He could make me feel like I was the only thing that mattered."

Douglas remained in frequent demand as a speaker and recited Robert Burns at Burns nights. He treasured a rare, antique Burns volume that Shirley had bought for him in London. He used the book so heavily—it accompanied him on countless trips, was read and reread in thousands of hotel rooms—that the cover began to fall off. Unconcerned with its value to collectors, Douglas had it rebound in a nice sturdy new cover and threw away the old one.

In 1979 Douglas, who had been the first senior Canadian politician to call for the recognition of Communist China at the United Nations, led a delegation of the Douglas-Coldwell Foundation, including NDP politicians, co-op leaders, and labour leaders, to the People's Republic. At that time, entry into China was very limited. Travel conditions in that country at the time were less comfortable than some of the delegates were accustomed to, and a large contingent felt they would like to return home early. They quietly devised a plan to cut the trip short when the group was to pass through Shanghai. Douglas caught wind of this plot and icily announced that the entire group was going to gather for a brief "tea talk." At the appointed time, he advised his colleagues of the great honour that they were being given as guests of China and declared that no one would be leaving early. The mutiny quashed, the delegation continued beyond Shanghai. Douglas marvelled at what he saw of China and gushed about the trip for years afterwards.

In the last days of Trudeau's government, Douglas was made a Companion of the Order of Canada. Later, Prime Minister Brian Mulroney made Douglas a privy councillor. He began to work on a book, *A New Democracy*, which was never completed. The book's outline furthered the themes of Douglas's life, calling for public planning, the considered use of new knowledge and technology, and the building of a co-operative society predicated on the welfare of its people.

In 1981 Tommy Douglas was diagnosed with cancer. He remained active, going for brisk daily walks and taking lunch every day at the Colonnade Restaurant on Metcalfe Street in Ottawa. Of aging and illness he complained, "I find it takes longer and longer to do less and less." Everything was still measured in terms of work to be done. About the same time he learned in conversation that Shirley did not know much about self-defence. He found this to be ridiculous, and gave her an impromptu lesson in disabling an attacker, which began by showing her how to strike an assailant on the bridge of the nose. On all fronts he remained himself, battling for good, ready to meet the enemy.

Douglas spoke at the NDP national convention in 1983, which coincided with the fiftieth anniversary of the Regina

Manifesto. His health was poor, but the fire burned brightly. He reminisced a little, and mostly looked toward the work ahead, calling on the delegates to do their utmost to build a humane, prosperous, and peaceful world. It would not be easy. He said, "The growth and development of the New Democratic Party must never allow us to forget our roots. Don't sacrifice conviction for success. Don't ever give up on quality for quantity. In a movement like ours, as socialist movements around the world have demonstrated, we're not just interested in getting votes.... We are seeking to get people who are willing to dedicate their lives to building a different kind of society ... a society founded on the principles of concern for human well being and human welfare."

On a cold winter's day in early 1986, a frail Douglas summoned all his strength and dressed himself. He said that he wished to go to the parliamentary barber shop. Shirley took him, and the barbers and staff on the Hill made a great fuss over him. He was satisfied with this outing and returned home. This was to be the last time he ventured out. Several weeks later, on February 24, 1986, Douglas passed away at his home in Ottawa. Churches and assembly halls across the country were filled with mourners, as Canadians of all political stripes offered their tributes. One could almost hear Douglas encouraging those around him to continue, with words he had once spoken: "No matter how many setbacks there may be along the road, you may be sure that some day the right and just will prevail. It will prevail simply because it is right and just."

Douglas would not have been surprised to know that even as he was writing the last chapters in the book of his political life, another document was being clandestinely compiled in parallel. In 2005 the Canadian Press reporter Jim Bronskill made an Access to Information request for the RCMP dossier on Tommy Douglas. Heavily censored portions of the eleven-hundred-page file were released, but hundreds of pages remain sealed at the time of this writing. Apparently the RCMP, and later the Canadian Security Intelligence Service (CSIS), were monitoring him from his days as a preacher in Weyburn. They were concerned about his connections with communism. His repeated public renunciations and his condemnations of communism had not reassured them. If any incriminating evidence about Douglas, a vocal critic of many sitting governments, had been obtained over the course of four decades of surveillance, it's hard to imagine that it wouldn't have been used against him at the time and that we wouldn't have heard about it by now.

At this writing, a Federal Court hearing is pending. CSIS continues to block full access to the Douglas files, saying in its affidavit, "Sources may still be active.... Some of the investigations are entities that remain of interest for many decades." Paul Champ, the lawyer representing the Canadian Press in this matter, has suggested that federal agencies are trying to avoid embarrassment rather than guard state secrets, and that they "engaged in certain surveillance practices they now find embarrassing." Wesley Wark, a University of Toronto security expert who wrote an affidavit in support of greater disclosure of the Douglas files, said, "The notion that once-sensitive security and intelligence records remain sensitive for eternity is a patent absurdity."

Douglas always knew that powerful vested interests tended to act as if they were above the law, and that was why there was a need for government transparency, accountability, and the protection of civil rights. He was not paranoid. He knew how the world worked. Once, at an anti-war rally in the 1970s, Anne Scotton, daughter of the NDP national secretary Cliff Scotton, noticed that someone was taking photos of her, Douglas, and others at the rally. She pointed it out to Douglas, who said, "Well, don't you know, they're making a file on you, and me, and everyone here." If he had known that he had been under surveillance for forty years, he might have been outraged but not surprised. It would have confirmed his view that some powerful people are willing to use almost any means, including secret files and the hiding of their activities, to maintain power. It would have reaffirmed his belief that those who believe in humanity must confront those who abuse power by devoting themselves to building societies of openness, co-operation, and justice.

SOURCES

Badgley, Wolfe. *Doctors' Strike: Medical Care and Conflict in Saskatchewan.* New York: Atherton Press, 1967.

Baptist Archives. Baptist Union of Western Canada, Year Book, 1922.

Barootes, Efstathios. Quoted in *Maclean's,* December 22, 1996.

Blakeney, Allan. Author interview, March 29, 2010.

Broadbent, Ed. Author interview, October 29, 2010.

Brown, Lorne A., Joseph K. Roberts, and Lorne W. Warnock. *Saskatchewan Politics from Left to Right '44 to '99.* Regina: Hinterland Publications, 1999.

Bryden, P.E. *Planners and Politicians: Liberal Politics and Social Policy, 1957–1968.* Montreal and Kingston: McGill-Queen's University Press, 1997.

CCF. *Planning for Freedom: A Presentation of Principles, Policy, & Program.* Ontario CCF: 1944.

CCF Papers, Saskatoon, 6, no. 5. TCD radio broadcast transcript, December 14, 1943.

Cohen, Andrew. *Lester B. Pearson,* Extraordinary Canadians series. Toronto: Penguin Group (Canada), 2009.

Douglas, Shirley. Author interviews, February 19, March 18, and November 27, 2010.

Douglas, Tommy. *Speeches of Tommy Douglas* (collection of public speeches and broadcasts on DVD). Ottawa: Douglas-Coldwell Foundation.

———. Quoted in the *Calgary Herald,* November 2, 1970.

———. Quoted in *The Vancouver Sun,* April 4, 1963.

———. Report of the provincial leader T.C. Douglas to the Eighth Annual CCF Convention, July 14–16, 1943.

———. *Debates and Proceedings,* Saskatchewan Legislature, 1961, Special Session, vol. 11, p. 96.

Falconer, Kenneth. "Tommy Douglas, 1930–1944." M.A. thesis, University of Regina, 1979.

Fines, Clarence. "The Impossible Dream." Unpublished memoir, 1981. Saskatchewan Archives.

Gibson, Graeme. Author interview, April 10, 2010.

Goldman, Lyn. Author interview, December 5, 2010.

Hawkins, Willard. *Castaways of Plenty: A Parable of Our Times.* Denver: Alan Swallow, 1964.

Hutchison, Bruce. *Maclean's,* August 1, 1944.

Johnson, A.W. *Dream No Little Dreams: A Biography of the Douglas Government of Saskatchewan, 1944–1961.* Toronto: University of Toronto Press, 2004.

Laycock, David. *Populism and Democratic Thought in the Canadian Prairies.* Toronto: University of Toronto Press, 1990.

Lewis, David, and Frank Scott. *Make This Your Canada*. Toronto: Central Canada Publishing Company, 1943.

Library and Archives Canada: TCD Papers, vol. 43, exchange of letters between TCD and Clinton White, 1975; TCD Papers, vol. 142, speech by TCD, September 10, 1958.

Lovick, L.D. *Tommy Douglas Speaks*. Lantzville: Oolichan Books, 1979.

Lower, A.R.M. *Colony to Nation*. Toronto: Longmans Green, 1946.

Margoshes, Dave. *Tommy Douglas: Building the New Society*. Montreal: XYZ Publishing, 1999.

McLellan, Richard. Author interview, August 3, 2010.

McNaught, Kenneth. *A Prophet in Politics: A Biography of J.S. Woodsworth*. Toronto: University of Toronto Press, 2001.

McLeod, Thomas H., and Ian McLeod. *Tommy Douglas: The Road to Jerusalem*. Calgary: Fifth House, 2004.

Mills, Allen. *Fool for Christ: The Political Thought of J.S. Woodsworth*. Toronto: University of Toronto Press, 1991.

Poliquin, Daniel. *René Lévesque*, Extraordinary Canadians series. Toronto: Penguin Group (Canada), 2009.

Rae, Bob. Author interview, March 29, 2010.

Romanow, Roy. Author interview, April 1, 2010.

Saskatchewan Archives: T.C. Douglas Economic Advisory and Planning Board Papers, R33.4, part III, minutes of joint cabinet–planning board meeting, September 9, 1946; TCD Ministerial Papers, file 20, TCD to Marjorie Barmby, May 30, 1951; Premier's Papers, file 130, Lewie Lloyd to TCD, September 23, 1956.

Scotton, Anne. Author interview, May 6, 2010.

Shackleton, Dorothy. *Tommy Douglas*. Toronto: McClelland & Stewart, 1975.

Spry, Robin. *Action: The October Crisis of 1970* (documentary). National Film Board of Canada, 1973.

Stewart, Walter. *The Life and Political Times of Tommy Douglas*. Toronto: McArthur & Company, 2003.

Sutherland, Kiefer. "Introducing the Tommy Douglas Showcase," NDP Convention, Quebec City, 2006.

Swerhone, Elise. *Tommy Douglas: Keeper of the Flame* (documentary). National Film Board of Canada, 1986.

Thomas, Lewis. *The Making of a Socialist: The Recollections of T.C. Douglas*. Edmonton: The University of Alberta Press, 1982.

Tulchinsky, Joan. Correspondence with author. October and November 2010.

United Church Archives. *Methodist Acts and Proceedings*.

United Church Archives. "The New Deal and The New Party," Salem Bland Papers, Toronto. Address 1913.

Weyburn Review, October 3, 1935.

Woodsworth, J.S. "The Holy City, 1916," in *Towards Socialism* (pamphlet). Ontario Woodsworth Memorial Foundation, 1958.

Zakuta, Leo. *A Protest Movement Becalmed: A Study of the CCF.* Toronto: University of Toronto Press, 1964.

ACKNOWLEDGMENTS

I am grateful to Shirley Douglas, Bob Rae, Ed Broadbent, Allan Blakeney, Roy Romanow, Richard McLellan, Anne Scotton, Lyn Goldman, and Graeme Gibson, who generously made time to talk to me about their recollections of Tommy Douglas. Shirley was especially welcoming and open in sharing with me her memories of her father. Through these interviews I was able to consider him in a personal as well as a political and historical light. I would also like to thank Joan Tulchinsky for her correspondence with me regarding her father.

My understanding of Tommy Douglas has benefited throughout from Thomas McLeod and Ian McLeod's definitive biography, *Tommy Douglas: The Road to Jerusalem*, and from Dorothy Shackleton's comprehensive work, *Tommy Douglas*. A wonderful series of conversations between Douglas and the journalist Chris Higginbotham are recorded in Lewis H. Thomas's book *The Making of a Socialist: The Recollections of T.C. Douglas*, and provided many of the longer quotations that introduce each chapter of this book. Al Johnson's *Dream No Little Dreams* afforded insight into the mechanisms of the Douglas government in Saskatchewan. The staff at the Library and Archives Canada in Ottawa were unfailingly helpful in assisting me to access their large collection of archival material on Douglas, and Doug Massey graciously welcomed me at the Douglas-Coldwell Foundation.

Thank you to John Ralston Saul and Diane Turbide, for asking me to write this book and trusting me with this important topic, and to my editor, Jonathan Webb, for his perceptive contributions to the manuscript. My friend Kenneth Wace reviewed the text and improved it with his frank opinions. I am appreciative of Alison Reid's copy edit. My indefatigable agents, Anne McDermid and Martha Magor Webb, were supportive at every stage. Finally, and crucially, I am deeply grateful to my wife, Margarita, for encouraging me in this project, and helping me with some tricky decisions regarding its final contours. To all my family, and especially my children, I owe a debt of gratitude for accepting the life of this project in our house.

1904   Thomas (Tommy) Clement Douglas is born in
        Falkirk, Scotland, October 20.

1910   Tommy's father, Thomas (Tom), and his uncle
        Willie Douglas sail to Canada and settle in
        Winnipeg.

1911   Tommy, his mother, Anne, and his sister, Nan,
        join Tom in Winnipeg.

1911–14 Tommy suffers from recurrent osteomyelitis in
        his right leg, resulting in lengthy hospital
        admissions.

1914   Dr. R. Smith, a renowned orthopedic surgeon,
        offers to operate on Tommy's leg at no cost as a
        teaching case and saves it from amputation.

1914–18 The Douglas family returns to Scotland and
        settles in Glasgow for the duration of the war
        while Tom serves with the ambulance corps.

1919   The family returns to Winnipeg in January.

        Winnipeg General Strike: Douglas and his
        friend Mark Talnicoff witness the violent

dispersal of striking workers on "Bloody Saturday," June 21.

Douglas begins a five-year apprenticeship in the printing trade.

1922   Douglas wins the lightweight boxing championship of Manitoba, retaining the title in 1923.

1924   With Mark Talnicoff, Douglas enrols in Brandon College, Manitoba, to study theology.

1927   Douglas assumes the ministry at Carberry Presbyterian Church, while still a student minister. Irma Dempsey is a teenage member of the congregation at Carberry.

1928   Irma Dempsey attends Brandon College as a piano student in the faculty of music; Douglas courts her.

1930   Calvary Baptist Church in Weyburn, Saskatchewan, chooses Douglas over Stanley Knowles as its minister.

Douglas and Irma Dempsey are married and move to Weyburn.

1931   Douglas pursues but does not complete studies toward a Ph.D. degree at the University of

Chicago as a part-time student; while in Chicago, he visits the "hobo jungles" created by the Depression.

Police kill three striking coal miners and wound more than twenty in Estevan, Saskatchewan; the wounded are taken to Weyburn.

1932   J.S. Woodsworth introduces Douglas to labour leader M.J. Coldwell.

The Co-operative Commonwealth Federation (CCF) is formed under the leadership of J.S. Woodsworth.

1933   At the national convention in Regina in July, a detailed policy statement, later known as the Regina Manifesto, is written.

Douglas completes an M.A. program (by corre-spondence) at McMaster University with his thesis on "The Problems of the Subnormal Family."

1934   Birth of Shirley Douglas, first daughter of Tommy and Irma.

Douglas runs as a CCF candidate in the provincial election and loses to the Liberal candidate.

1935   Douglas runs as a CCF candidate in the federal election and wins a seat as MP for Weyburn.

1936   Douglas travels to Switzerland, Spain, and Germany as a delegate to the World Youth Congress.

1939   On the outbreak of the Second World War, Douglas volunteers for service with the South Saskatchewan Regiment; he trains when Parliament is not in session and rises to rank of captain.

1942   Douglas is elected leader of Saskatchewan CCF, replacing George Williams; Clarence Fines is elected president of the party.

1944   The CCF takes forty-seven of fifty-two seats in Saskatchewan, sweeping the Liberals from power, and introducing the first socialist government in North America.

The CCF government makes good on its promises of reform, passing seventy-six pieces

of legislation between October 19 and
November 10.

1945   As the Second World War nears its end,
Douglas spends three months in Europe,
visiting troops.

1946   Joan Douglas, an adopted daughter, joins the
Douglas family.

At Douglas's invitation, George Cadbury
advises his government on introducing socialist
measures in a prudently run mixed economy.

1947   The CCF government enacts the Saskatchewan
Bill of Rights.

Universal hospital insurance is introduced in
Saskatchewan.

1948   The new Public Service Act introduces radical
reforms in Saskatchewan's civil service.

The Saskatchewan Arts Board is created, the
first institution of its kind in North America.

1949   The rural electrification program begins in
Saskatchewan.

1960   The Douglas government in Saskatchewan sets
up its Advisory Planning Committee on

Medical Care to advise on steps leading to the introduction of medicare in the province.

Proposed medicare legislation is a key issue in the contentious Saskatchewan provincial election in March.

1961   In August Douglas steps down from the leadership of the provincial party to become leader of the newly created federal New Democratic Party (NDP).

Woodrow Lloyd replaces Douglas as provincial premier and passes the Medical Care Insurance Act.

1962   Saskatchewan doctors go on strike in protest against medicare legislation; Lord Taylor's arbitration brings the strike to an end on July 23.

Douglas fails to win a seat in Regina in the June federal election; he subsequently wins a by-election in the British Columbia riding of Burnaby-Coquitlam, and the family relocates to B.C.

1964   The Hall Commission report to the federal government recommends the adoption of uni-